IMAGES

of America

WELCH

ON THE COVER: Former West Virginia governor Cecil Underwood tips his cane to the crowd gathered at the reviewing stand on McDowell Street during the McDowell County Centennial Parade in May 1958. Underwood was riding a 1916 Model T Ford, one of several Model T Fords owned by F. E. Surface, owner of Surface Banana, a regional produce wholesaler. His fellow passenger was West Virginia's first congresswoman, Elizabeth Kee. Surface was driving this car while his son Charles Surface appears in the passenger seat. F. E. Surface had eight antique cars that he took to parades throughout the region. Another of Surface's sons, William "Wish" Surface, and his daughter, Evelyn Linkous, are the driver and passenger of the 1921 Model T behind the lead Surface car. (Courtesy of the West Virginia Room Collection of the McDowell County Library.)

IMAGES
of America

WELCH

William R. "Bill" Archer

ARCADIA
PUBLISHING

Published by Arcadia Publishing
Charleston, South Carolina

Library of Congress Catalog Card Number: 2006925656

For all general information contact Arcadia Publishing at:
Telephone 843-853-2070
Fax 843-853-0044
E-mail sales@arcadiapublishing.com
For customer service and orders:
Toll-Free 1-888-313-2665

Visit us on the Internet at www.arcadiapublishing.com

*I dedicate this book to my mother-in-law, Marjorie Cozart,
whose personal example of faith, humility, and determination
serve as a constant inspiration to me.*

CONTENTS

ACKNOWLEDGMENTS

This is my fifth book in Arcadia Publishing's Images of America series, and as with each of my previous projects, I owe a great debt of gratitude to my wife, Evonda Archer, for her steadfast support, emotional guidance, and proofreading skills. Many, many people helped with this project. I would like to express my thanks to Welch mayor Martha Moore, who has helped me appreciate the city she loves since I started reporting on Welch in 1986. I would also like to thank Donna Morgan, Welch librarian, who graciously opened the West Virginia Room Collection to me. The West Virginia Room Collection contained several archival photographs and images from the 1958 McDowell centennial edition of the *Welch Daily News* that were useful in compiling this collection. I would also like to thank Jay and Julia Chapman, who allowed me to work with their Huger Collection to make this work special.

I would also like to thank Rev. Tim Hairston, Birdie Beavers, Louise Warden, Ken Davidson, Ruth and Cecil Surratt, Bill Kell, David McNeil, Mel Grubb, Shirley Ofsa, Jack Caffrey, Debbie Lewis, H. C. "Kit" Lewis, Garnett Edwards, Rick Murensky, Deborah Rushbrook, Evelyn Linkous, Robert Mrazek, Kathy Saddler, Charlie Cornett, Josephine Cavallo, Mike and Martha Carol Calloway, Lefty Guard, Carlton Viar, Jim Fields, Sandy Miller, Pete Ballard, John Nelson, Allen Roberts, Randy Deason, Tom Colley, the readers of the *Bluefield Daily Telegraph*, Ronnie Coe, Jaimee Gauldin, and Dr. Frank England.

INTRODUCTION

Perhaps more than any other place on earth, the city of Welch is a force of nature. In spite of the fact that there is very little level ground to build on, Welch became the mid-20th-century capital of North America's coal energy empire. During the first half of the 20th century, the city experienced rapid growth as thousands of Eastern European immigrants poured past the Statue of Liberty in New York City and, within hours, traveled straight to the coalfields where they found a true land of opportunity where color, national origin, and faith were tolerated, while ambition, sweat, and drive were venerated. For many immigrants, the 10-hour trip from New York to Welch represented the greatest step they would ever take toward establishing a permanent place for their families in the New World. For African American families, the journey from the Carolinas and Virginia into the southern West Virginia coalfields was much shorter in terms of duration, but equally important in terms of economic and social freedom. Throughout its history, Welch epitomized the concept of the mixing bowl of nations.

Yet there is also a very powerful component of Welch that almost defies the very rules of nature that have governed the city's development. The surrounding mountains serve as an underlying sub-current that continues to drive the city's progress. Welch is located in a place where the Elkhorn Creek and Browns Creek join the Tug Fork of the Big Sandy River. All three bodies of water are swift-moving mountain streams that cut through a section of the Allegheny Mountain Range that resembles parts of the European Alps, according to a McDowell County native son, Lt. Gen. Robert Gray (U.S. Army, retired). The flat land in the heart of Welch is barely broad enough to hold a football field, but enterprising architects, engineers, and builders found a way to cram more than 6,000 residents into the tiny patch of real estate. Despite an onslaught of unchecked mountain flash floods that routinely devastated the downtown, Welch citizens persistently found ways to thrive in an environment where no dream was beyond reach.

The list of Americans with direct connections to Welch is incredible. During the late 1700s, Robert Morris, the so-called "financier of the American Revolution" acquired a half-million acres with Welch at its heart. Morris speculated on the land's mineral and natural wealth, but died a pauper before he could exploit it. Michael Bouvier, great-grandfather of Jacqueline Bouvier Kennedy Onassis, was the next to try owning the region in the 1830s. Bouvier was lured by the region's untouched virgin hardwood forest, but the Bouvier investment took time to realize a profitable return.

McDowell County was founded in 1858 as one of the last counties created in Virginia before the start of the American Civil War. The war devastated Virginia's agrarian economy, prompting postwar entrepreneurs to embrace the industrial age to stand as Virginia's salvation. Jed Hotchkiss, a Staunton, Virginia, geologist and Gen. Stonewall Jackson's mapmaker, promoted the development of the southern West Virginia coalfields as a means to resurrect the Old Dominion. In 1873, he hired Capt. Isaiah A. Welch, a former officer in the Army of Northern Virginia, to undertake a survey of the Pocahontas Coalfields. Although Welch didn't live there, on July 12, 1894, the City of Welch was named in his honor.

During the following decades, the city of Welch grew dramatically. Only 78 citizens cast votes in the city's first election, but by the late 1950s, the city's population had swelled to more than 6,600 people. In keeping with the moniker of capital of the Free State of McDowell, the people of Welch have maintained a fiercely independent streak in good times and in bad. The city's patriotic zeal is incredible, and the guest speakers at the annual Veterans Day Parade in Welch include Presidents Harry Truman and Lyndon Johnson, as well as scores of prominent political and military leaders. The patriotic spirit of Welch has remained unchanged for more than a century.

At the same time, celebrity personalities such as the great historical drama playwright Kermit Hunter and comedian Steve Harvey share Welch as a common heritage. Hunter was born in McDowell County on October 2, 1910, and grew up in the city, and Harvey was born in Welch on January 17, 1956, and spent the first five years of his life growing up in Gary, a nearby town.

The city of Welch suffered a devastating blow on May 2, 2002, when the Elkhorn Creek and Tug Fork floodwaters swamped the community beneath several feet of water and mud, but that flood along with the July 8, 2001, flood did not diminish the spirit of the city. Mayor Martha Moore and the Welch City Council have maintained a steady drive to work with local entrepreneurs, as well as state and federal agencies, on a citywide renaissance program aimed at saving the historic charm of the city while positioning the community for growth in the future. This book is dedicated to that ongoing effort.

One

BIRTH OF A CITY

GEE HA. Ed Brewster is shown bringing his rig up to the old Flat Top Bottling Works that was situated on McDowell Street where the American Legion Hall is now located. (Courtesy of Louise Warden.)

THE GREAT SURVEYOR. This rare portrait of Capt. Isaiah A. Welch shows the coalfield developer in the twilight years of his life. Welch was born November 3, 1824, in Doddridge County, Virginia (now West Virginia), and died in St. Albans, West Virginia, on February 15, 1902. Welch remained loyal to Virginia after the Old Dominion seceded from the Union and served during the Civil War as assistant quartermaster in the 13th Battalion, Virginia Light Infantry. He was part of an all-volunteer force assembled in Richmond, Virginia, in February 1864 to defend the city from Union general J. A. Dahlgren's raid. Welch resigned his commission July 16, 1864, and represented Kanawha County, West Virginia, in the Virginia General Assembly. The Virginia General Assembly did not recognize West Virginia's June 20, 1863, birth in 1864. In 1873, Welch was hired by Jed Hotchkiss to conduct a survey of the Pocahontas Coalfields. Welch's survey became the blueprint for development of the southern West Virginia/southwestern Virginia coalfields and earned him the appreciation of the founding fathers of Welch, who named the city in his honor. (Courtesy of Birdie Beavers.)

FINAL RESTING PLACE. Isaiah A. Welch was laid to rest in the Oak Hill Cemetery in the Freeman community, near Bramwell, Mercer County, West Virginia. The obituary writer in the *Bluefield Daily Telegraph* characterized Welch as "the most widely known man in the field," who was "universally esteemed. The town of Welch was named in his honor." (Courtesy of Birdie Beavers.)

BIG HOUSE ON THE HILL. The Col. William Leckie home, shown, was built in the early 20th century on Maple Avenue in Welch on the hill overlooking the location where the Welch Norfolk and Western passenger station would be built. Leckie was one of McDowell County's early coal barons who developed mines at the headwaters of the Tug Fork of the Big Sandy River in what is now called Gary Hollow. The town of Leckie is named in his honor. Colonel Leckie is shown at

the center of this picture seated on the sidewalk steps to his home, and his wife, Annie Leckie, is seated about midway up the steps to the porch. Several other Leckie children and relatives are also shown here, including Andrew Leckie, Nellie (Leckie) Kell, William Leckie, Douglas Leckie, Miriam Leckie, Margaret Baldwin, and Thornton Kell. The photograph was taken sometime in the second decade of the 20th century. (Courtesy of William Kell.)

SOCIABLE POLITICS. This saloon located at the corner of Wyoming and Railroad Streets in Welch served as the town's first courthouse. (Courtesy of Louise Warden.)

THE RAIL THING. The Norfolk and Western passenger station, shown in this photograph from 1900, was a focal point of activity in Welch. Only a few of the people pictured here were identified in the 1958 centennial edition of the *Welch Daily News*. Those identified included the girl in the foreground on the platform, Mrs. Robert M. Kyle, the man directly behind her, Col. Bill Eubank, and the third man from the right on the platform, Macon W. Hudson. (Courtesy of Louise Warden.)

FASHIONABLE. The C. D. Brewster Company store, shown in this 1904 photograph, was located on upper McDowell Street in the heart of downtown Welch. The store offered a wide array of merchandise to the growing community. From left to right are Reece Evans, C. D. Brewster, Dr. S. A. Daniel, and Bob Brewster. (Courtesy of Louise Warden.)

McDOWELL STREET. This photograph of McDowell Street looking west was taken in the early 1900s and shows the old Tug River Hotel, First National Bank, and Welch Meat Market along with other old businesses. The image dates from a time when the street had not yet been paved. (Courtesy of Louise Warden.)

15

ARRIVAL OF THE IRON HORSE. This 1892 photograph shows the first steam locomotive to arrive in Welch. Isaiah A. Welch surveyed the coalfields in 1873, and the Southwest Virginia Improvement Company started shipping coal from Pocahontas, Virginia, in 1883. The Norfolk and Western Railway made it to Welch in 1892. (Courtesy of Louise Warden.)

ONE IF BY LAND. Most people arrived in Welch by rail, but horse-and-buggy transportation provided a needed link to get goods and services to the people as evidenced in this mid-20th-century photograph from the Huger Collection. The identities of the men pictured are not known. (Courtesy of Jay Chapman.)

16

BUILDING BOOM. Growth in Welch during the early 1900s followed the narrow streams and riverbeds and the Norfolk and Western Railway tracks but soon spread to the steep mountainsides. The photograph here shows development near Elkhorn Creek near present-day Howard Street. (Courtesy of the West Virginia Room Collection, McDowell County Public Library.)

WELCH DAWN. Welch experienced dramatic growth in the decade that followed its 1894 charter, as can be seen in this January 1903 photograph of the city looking up the Tug Fork of the Big Sandy River. Note the McDowell County Courthouse in the photograph to the left. (Courtesy of Grubb Photo Service.)

BIG ELKHORN. This early-20th-century photograph of Welch on both sides of the Elkhorn Creek shows the old First Methodist Church under construction on the right and only a few homes on Maple Avenue to the far right. The old swinging bridge crosses Elkhorn Creek near the present location of the bridge near Welch City Hall. (Courtesy of Grubb Photo Service.)

OLD SCHOOL. The class of 1910 is shown here in this photograph of Welch's first school. The school was located on Maple Avenue. George E. Rhodes was the first principal. Included here are Superintendent ? Riggs, Carl Hudson, Mrs. R. M. Kyle, Lena Tinch, Gladys Hall, Sallie Shell, Pearl Stultz, Tofa Shell, Mary Dickerson, Bill Tabor Johnson, Fred Mitchell, Ernest Kyle, and George E. Rhodes. (Courtesy of the West Virginia Room Collection, McDowell County Library.)

TO YOUR HEALTH. The groundbreaking ceremony for the Miners Hospital No. 1 is shown here. The hospital was formally opened on January 15, 1902. In recent years, the hospital has been renamed Welch Community Hospital. (Courtesy of Grubb Photo Service.)

VOLUNTEERS. The Welch Volunteer Fire Department is shown here *c.* 1919. The firefighters shown here from left to right are Felix Barker on rear bumper of the fire truck; David Plunkett, Jess Stultz, and Stopper Thompson standing; Chester Harman and A. V. Dennen seated on the running board; John W. Blakely and Reese Paisley in the seat; and Reece Helmondollar and Dr. G. Dewey Mitchell on the hood. (Courtesy of Grubb Photo Service.)

Two

SPIRIT BORN OF BATTLE

EVER READY. Several unidentified members of the armed forces, the Salvation Army, the American Legion, and civic leaders are shown here in this Huger Collection photograph of a World War II–era air raid shelter in front of the old First National Bank building on McDowell Street. Although Welch was hundreds of miles inland, it was believed to be a potential target during the war because of its strategic importance in the nation's coal industry. (Courtesy of Jay Chapman.)

LOVE A PARADE. McDowell County people have an incredible passion for supporting the nation's military that extends back to the foundation of the city and through to the present day. The photograph here shows what appears to be a 1930s vintage parade through the city streets. (Courtesy of the City of Welch.)

HEY, GOOD LOOKING. A group of men are shown here demonstrating their fashionable attributes in this parade photograph from the Huger Collection. (Courtesy of Jay Chapman.)

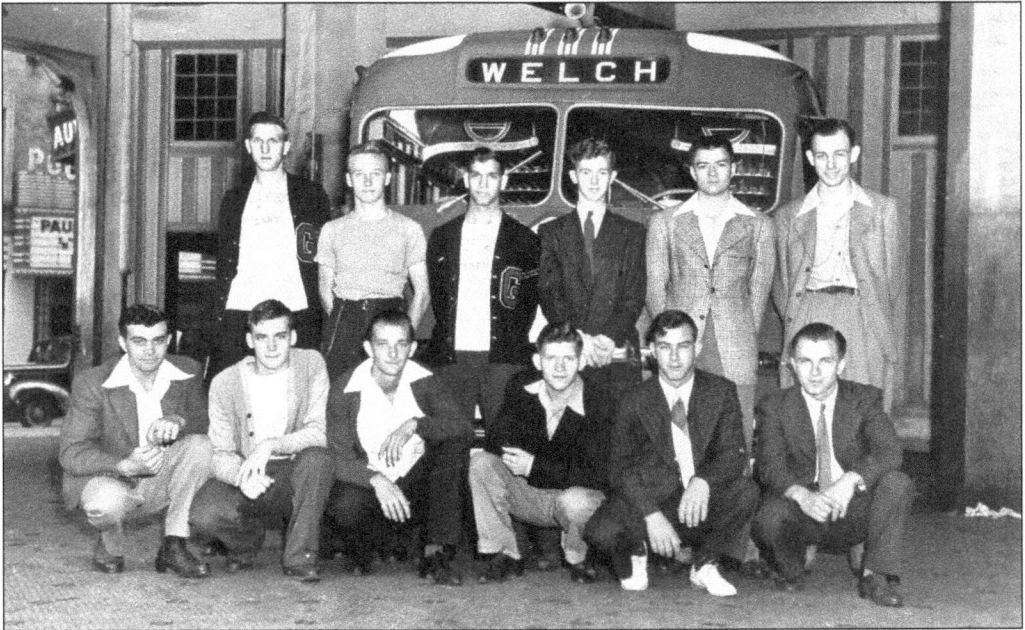

RECRUITS. This Huger Collection photograph taken at the old bus terminal in downtown Welch shows a group of recruits preparing to leave for service in the military. Although not all of the identities of the men are now known, Tracy Stewart is shown in the first row at the far left, according to Kathy Sadler. (Courtesy of Jay Chapman.)

IN MEMORIAL. The Welch World War I Memorial was the first memorial built in the United States to honor the service of soldiers who fought in World War I. Hassel T. Hicks designed the memorial. (Courtesy of Louise Warden.)

RECOGNITION. Hazel Hicks (left), widow of Welch World War I Memorial architect Hassel T. Hicks, is shown here being recognized by the City of Welch. Mayor W. B. Swope is seated here with ? Hawthorne and Sam Polon. (Courtesy of the City of Welch.)

SCRAP METAL DRIVE. The two young men shown here in this Huger Collection photograph—Bill Barris on the left and Blake Shrout—are apparently collecting metal for a scrap metal drive. The lads are shown on Railroad Avenue near the old Welch depot on the Norfolk and Western Railway. Pete Ballard helped track down the identities of the young men. (Courtesy of Jay Chapman.)

OVER THERE. The support for America's military is near legendary in McDowell County and Welch. An unidentified sailor, nurse, and soldier are shown marching across the railroad crossing on McDowell Street with the First National Bank building in the background. The annual Veterans Day Parade in Welch continues to draw crowds in the hundreds and, perhaps, the thousands. (Courtesy of the West Virginia Room Collection, McDowell County Public Library.)

PRIMED AND READY. Welch took its strategic role in the national defense seriously as can be seen in this World War II vintage photograph from the Huger Collection of a Civil Defense team meeting. The identities of the people in the photograph are unknown. (Courtesy of Jay Chapman.)

ANTLERS IN THE TREETOPS. While young men and women from Welch volunteered for service in the military, civic and fraternal organizations at home demonstrated their undying support for veterans. This Huger Collection photograph shows a Loyal Order of the Moose float preparing to enter a Veterans Day Parade. (Courtesy of Jay Chapman.)

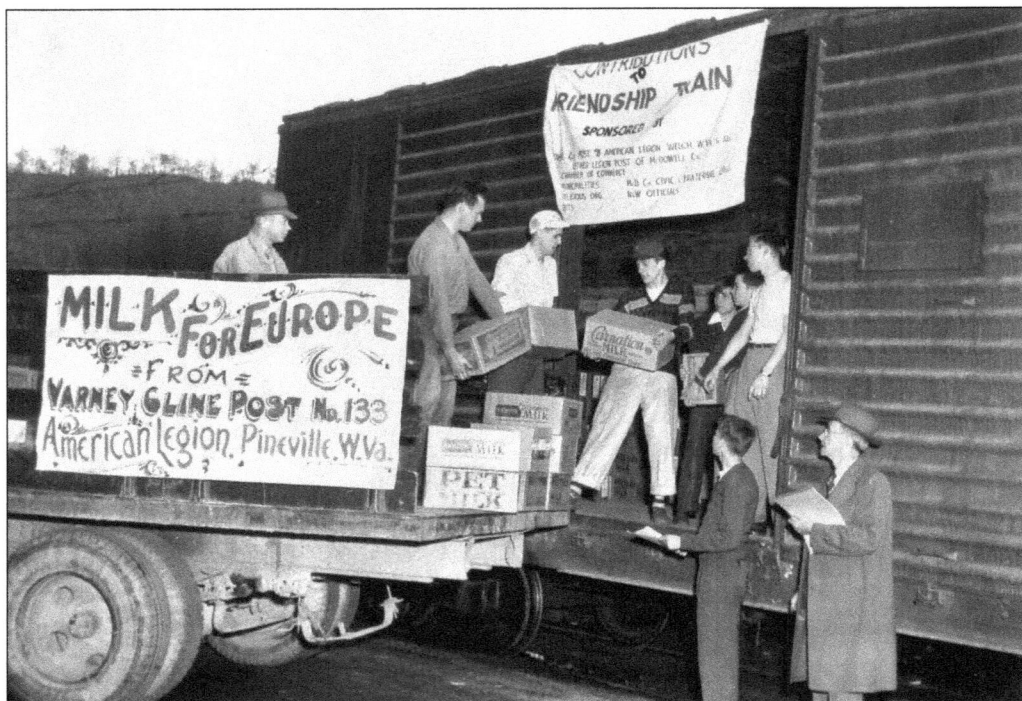

IN WAR AND IN PEACE. Volunteers are shown in this Huger Collection photograph loading milk from Pineville's Varney Cline Post No. 133 of the American Legion on a special "Friendship Train" to help the people of Europe who suffered through the ravages of World War II. (Courtesy of Jay Chapman.)

NAVAL WARFARE. The USS *Welch*, shown in this U.S. Navy photograph, was built in the Albania Engine and Machine Works, Portland, Oregon, and commissioned on July 13, 1943. (Courtesy of the West Virginia Room Collection, McDowell County Public Library.)

RAIN OR SHINE. Members of the McDowell County American Legion Auxiliary are shown in this Jim Christea photograph marching in a 1970s-era Veterans Day Parade in Welch. (Courtesy of the City of Welch.)

WHEREFORE ART THOU? Tony Romeo, a Korean War veteran, is shown here addressing a Veterans Day Parade in Welch. The Romeo family owned and operated Romeo Florist on Bank Street in Welch. (Courtesy of the City of Welch.)

BAND AID. A band is shown here performing at Welch's Blakely Field in this photograph from the Huger Collection. Blakely Field would eventually become the site of the Colonel W. E. Eubank Armory in Welch. Eubank served in the Spanish-American War and became commander of Company K, 2nd Infantry of the West Virginia National Guard organized in Welch on February 17, 1914. Blakely Field was named for John W. Blakely who served as mayor from 1924 to 1940. (Courtesy of Jay Chapman.)

PARADE REST. Joe Lassak is shown in the business suit at right, directing a marching band at an event held at Blakely Field in Welch. County and regional band competitions were held on the field for many years, but the field was also used for high-school football and served as the home of the Minor League Welch Miners professional baseball team. Col. W. E. Eubank organized Voiture 1171, La Societe 40&8, and that organization is named in his honor. His son, Brig. Gen. William E. Eubank, U.S. Air Force, served as commander of the 93rd Bombardment Wing and set distance flying records for the air force. (Courtesy of Shirley Ofsa.)

LIFETIME OF SERVICE. Legionnaires are shown here presenting a check to Robert Page and Welch Mayor W. B. Swope. From left to right are Kermit Werness, ? Lockhart, Buddy Herzburn, Page, and Swope. (Courtesy of the City of Welch.)

IN TRAINING. A group of McDowell County "Junior Deputies" is shown here in this 1970–1971 photograph. The young men served under Chief Field Deputy Jack Beavers (first row, second from left) and Sheriff Jack Christian (first row, second from right). (Courtesy of the City of Welch.)

OLD GLORY. Venerable Welch residents think this Huger Collection photograph was taken at a flag-raising ceremony in the vicinity of the present-day Mount View High School Golden Knights Stadium. (Courtesy of Jay Chapman.)

THE GOVERNATOR. Dr. Henry Drury Hatfield was born in 1876 in Mingo County but made a name for himself in McDowell County. He graduated from the University of Louisville School of Medicine in 1893 at age 17 and came to McDowell County in 1895 to serve as a surgeon for the Norfolk and Western Railway. He developed a practice devoted to serving "suffering humanity" and volunteered countless hours to creating Miners Hospital No. 1, now Welch Community Hospital. He started his career in public office as the Welch (Browns Creek) representative on the McDowell County Board of Education and won elections as a Republican state senator in 1908, senate president in 1910, and governor 1913–1917. At the end of his term as governor, he joined the Army Medical Corps and served as chief surgeon at the army's General Hospital in Detroit, Michigan. In 1928, he was elected U.S. senator from West Virginia. (Courtesy of Birdie Beavers.)

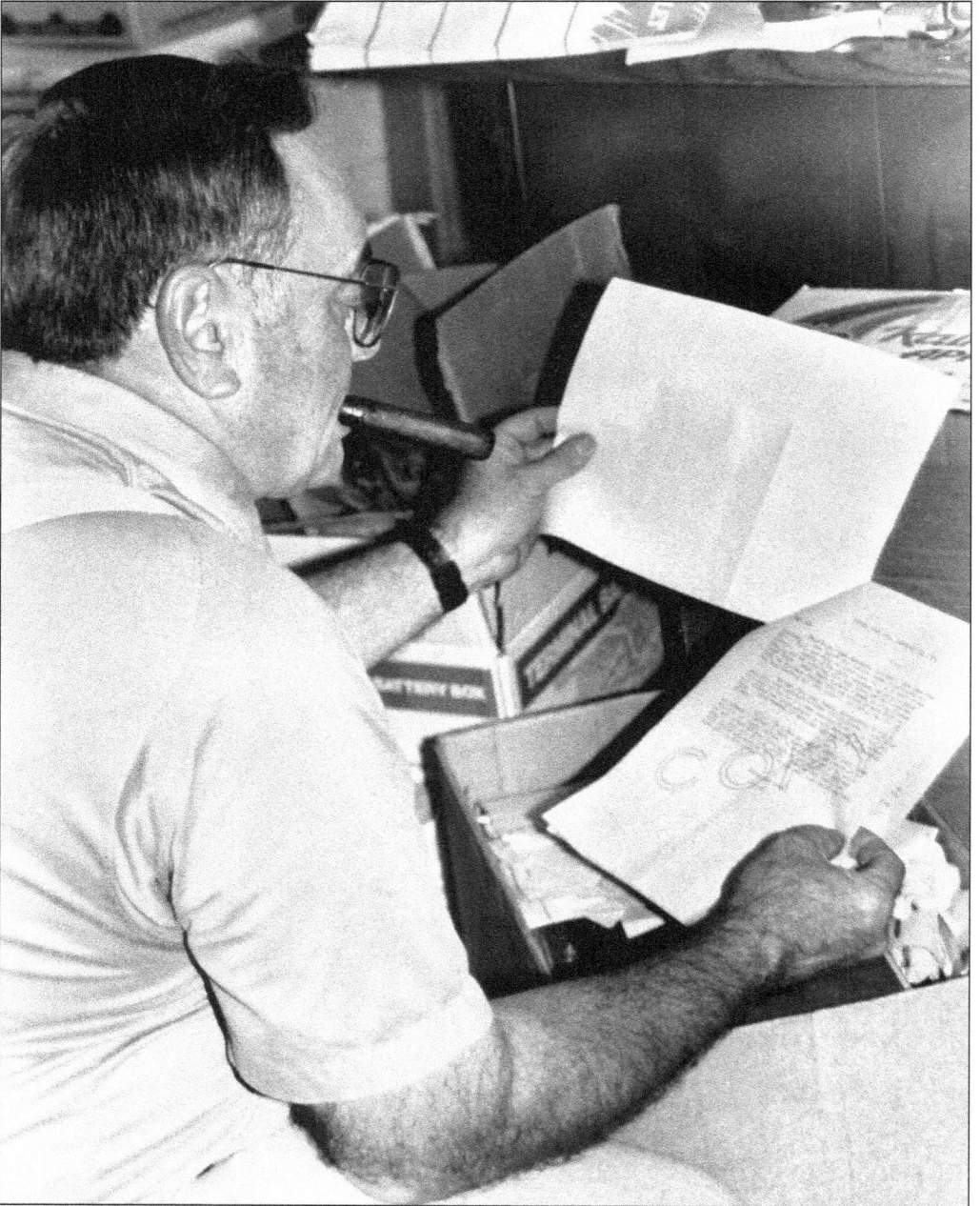

PAPER TREASURE. Welch businessman and civic leader H. C. "Kit" Lewis Jr. obtained a few boxes of documents in the summer of 1990 from Felts Transportation Company when H. C. Lewis Oil acquired the rival oil company. The boxes contained several personal correspondences between Thomas L. Felts and his field operatives during 1921. At that time, Felts was head of the Baldwin-Felts Detective Agency. Many of the letters were from Vernon Owens in Welch to Felts in Galax, Virginia. (Photograph by the author.)

MAN BEHIND THE STAR. T. L. Felts, shown here with rifle in hand at the 1912 capture of Floyd Allen in Hillsville, Virginia, built a detective agency that rivaled the better-known Pinkerton Detectives in terms of size and scope, but in 1920–1921, Felts took a personal interest in finding justice for his brothers, Albert and Lee Felts, who were killed along with seven other Baldwin-Felts detectives in a gun battle on May 19, 1920, in Matewan, West Virginia. Matewan Sheriff Sid Hatfield and one of his officers, Ed Chambers, were gunned down outside the McDowell County Courthouse on August 1, 1921. Hatfield, who was 26 at the time of his death, and Ed Chambers, 22, a Matewan police officer, were killed as they came to Welch to answer a subpoena related to a mine shoot-out in Mohawk earlier that same year. Hatfield was one of the leaders of the so-called "Matewan Massacre." (Photograph illustration by Evonda Archer.)

FINAL RESTING PLACE. After their deaths in Welch, the bodies of Hatfield and Chambers were buried in a cemetery in Kentucky near Matewan. The United Mine Workers of America recognized Hatfield for his service. (Photograph by Evonda Archer.)

TOP GUN. T. L. Felts, head of the Baldwin-Felts Detective Agency, traced the travels of Sid Hatfield after the Matewan Massacre in 1920 and appeared to maintain a keen interest in the case even after the Hatfield–Ed Chambers killings in Welch in 1921. Three Baldwin-Felts agents—C. E. Lively, George Pence, and William Salters—were arrested and charged with the murders. (Photograph illustration by Evonda Archer.)

SET IN STONE. The late Paul Lambert, longtime McDowell County clerk, is shown here in this 1990 photograph pointing to marks in the front of the McDowell County Courthouse believed to have been made by gunfire related to the August 1, 1921, shoot-out that claimed the lives of Sid Hatfield and Ed Chambers. (Photograph by the author.)

LIVING CLASSROOM. A group of children is shown here in this Huger Collection photograph seated on a grassy area outside the ivy-covered walls of the McDowell County Courthouse. The courthouse has been the site of many interesting events through its history. (Courtesy of Jay Chapman.)

RECORD RETENTION. The late Paul Lambert, former McDowell County clerk, is shown here in this 1990 photograph of an old room in the historic McDowell County Courthouse, pointing to the trial transcripts from the Ed Chambers murder trial in Welch that ended on December 17, 1921, with a not guilty verdict for the three Baldwin-Felts detectives, C. E. Lively, George Pence, and William Salters, who were charged with the murders of Chambers and Sid Hatfield. Lambert worked hard to draw attention to the county's efforts of trying to preserve the court records from significant trials throughout West Virginia history, but even though that same cause has been embraced by Lambert's successors, the records are still in peril. (Photograph by the author.)

Three

POWER OF NATURE

SNOW BEAUTIFUL. McDowell Street looks like a winter wonderland in this photograph from the Huger Collection. Note the Consolidated Bus Terminal on the right, which served hundreds of bus runs in and out of Welch each day. (Courtesy of Jay Chapman.)

WATER . . . WATER EVERYWHERE. This photograph shows the junction of Elkhorn Creek and the Tug Fork of the Big Sandy River in the March 25, 1935, flood. The first major flood that struck the Elkhorn Valley was on June 22, 1901, killing several coal miners and family members. Initial accounts of that flood told of a much higher death toll due to the fact that several bodies in a Northfork, West Virginia, cemetery were swept out of their graves in the flood. (Courtesy of the City of Welch.)

KNEE-DEEP IN TROUBLE. People are shown here milling through the floodwaters on McDowell Street in downtown Welch on March 25, 1935. The Tug Fork of the Big Sandy has spilled out of its banks several times since Welch was founded in 1894, but each time, the community has responded to adversity to rebuild the city. (Courtesy of the City of Welch.)

FEEL THE EXCITEMENT. The Welch High School Band is shown here marching on McDowell Street during a Veterans Day Parade. In spite of the frequent challenges, the spirit of Welch's citizens is never dimmed. (Courtesy of the City of Welch.)

PUT HER THERE, PAL. An unidentified legionnaire is shown in this photograph from the Huger Collection pointing to a wheelbarrow in the vicinity of the old Yeager Ford dealership. Note the (then) Welch Emergency Hospital in the background. (Courtesy of Jay Chapman.)

SNOWBOUND. Two unidentified transit drivers are shown here in this Huger Collection photograph with their snow-covered trucks parked appropriately in front of the White Front Café on McDowell Street. The trucks were likely headed to Center Auto Sales in Welch. (Courtesy of Jay Chapman.)

SKI COUNTRY. Two unidentified young ladies are shown here apparently enjoying the warmth of their home at the back of Woodland Court Apartments in Welch. This photograph from the Huger Collection shows a winter wonderland in the McDowell County capital. (Courtesy of Jay Chapman.)

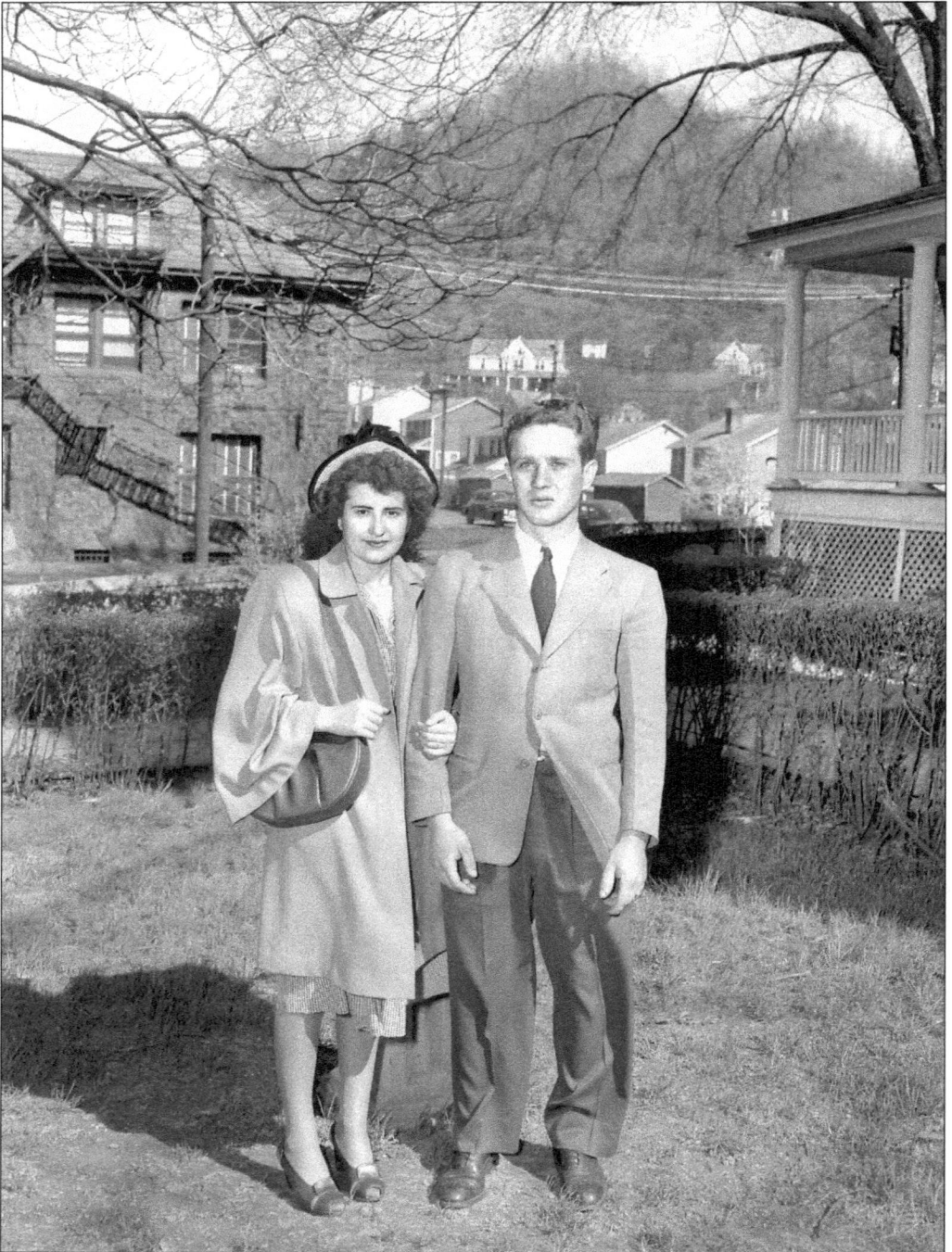

YOUNG LOVE. Josephine and Nick Cavallo met in Italy during World War II when Nick was in the service. It took a couple of years to work out the details, but on April 14, 1947, Mrs. Cavallo arrived in Welch after coming straight from Italy. The two were married at the Gary Catholic Church on April 19, 1947, where this photograph from the Huger Collection was taken. The Cavallos celebrated their 59th wedding anniversary in 2006. (Courtesy of Jay Chapman.)

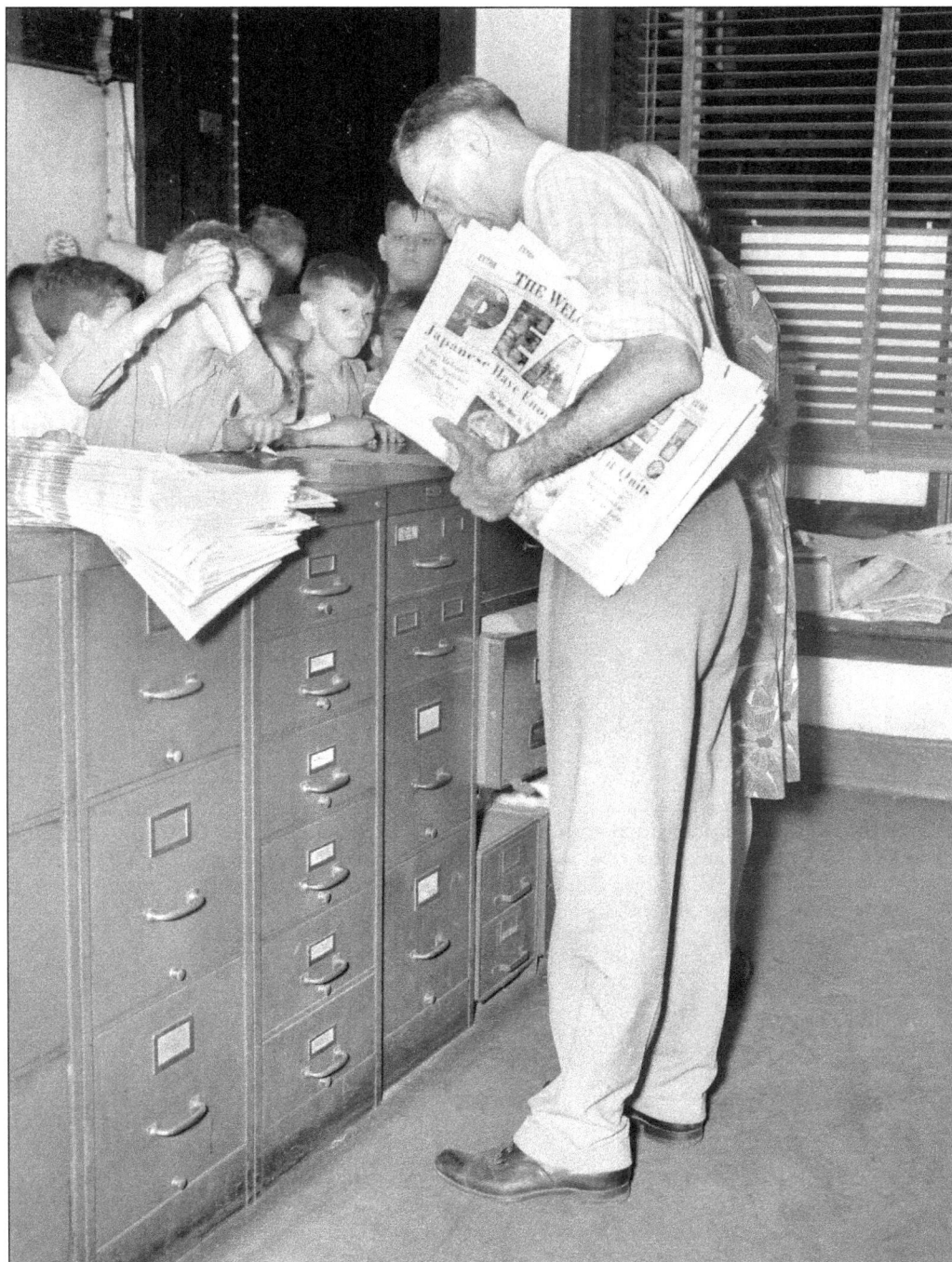

PEACE. W. R. "Will" Keyser, general manager of the *Welch Daily News*, is shown here in this Huger Collection photograph preparing to send a small army of newspaper boys out in the streets of Welch to carry the good news of the Japanese surrender on August 14, 1945. Pres. Harry Truman declared September 2, 1945, as V-J Day. Truman had been the Veterans Day speaker in Welch just four years earlier on November 11, 1941. (Courtesy of Jay Chapman.)

LET IT SNOW. Some unidentified children are shown here enjoying a little sleigh riding fun in this Huger Collection photograph of a snow scene on Maple Avenue in Welch. Life in the mountains of southern West Virginia is often unpredictable due in part to the constant vagaries of the weather. (Courtesy of Jay Chapman.)

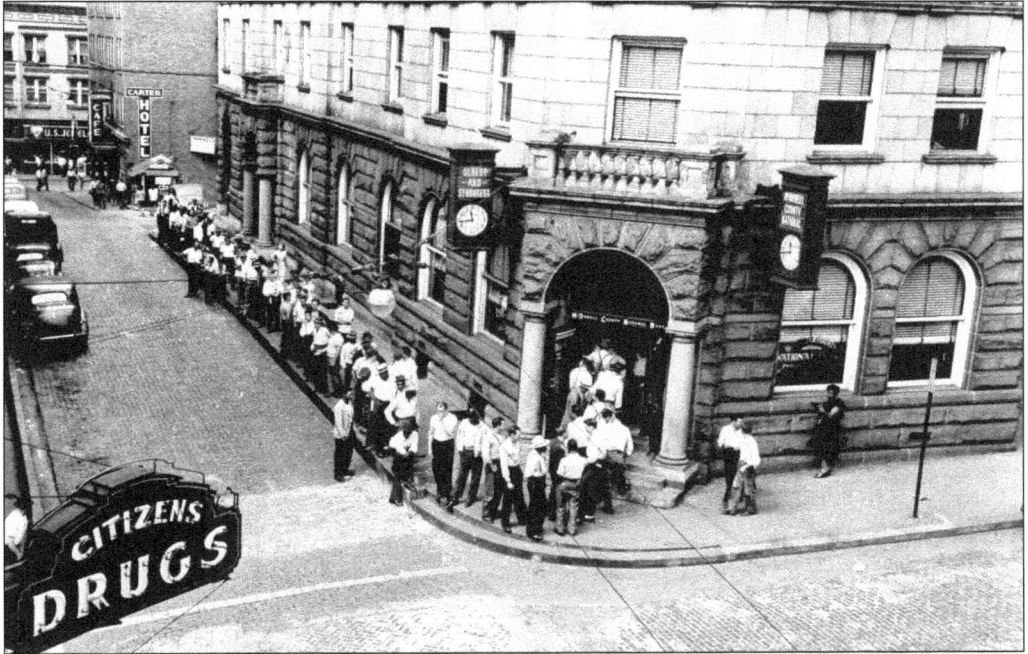

BANK ON IT. Payday at the McDowell County National Bank on Wyoming Street could be a rather lengthy proposition, as can be seen in this photograph from the Huger Collection. (Courtesy of Jay Chapman.)

WORK FORCE. This unidentified group of men appears to be gathered for a safety meeting in Welch. The diverse McDowell County workforce was responsible for extracting untold millions of tons of coal. (Courtesy of the City of Welch.)

MORE POWER TO YOU. The Welch Light, Heat and Power building, shown here on Wyoming Street in Welch, served as headquarters for a power distribution system that originated in 1902 and acquired used boilers from the U.S. Senate in 1904. The company started doing business with just 15 customers. (Courtesy of the West Virginia Room Collection, McDowell County Public Library.)

POWER ON THE MOVE. Welch Light, Heat and Power sold its business to Appalachian Power Company (APCO) on June 18, 1911, and APCO eventually moved its headquarters from Wyoming Street to the former Jones-Cornett Building on Howard Street, shown in this photograph from the Huger Collection. (Courtesy of Jay Chapman.)

POWERFUL PEOPLE. A group of Welch Appalachian Power Company employees is shown here posing near a service truck. The identities of the employees were not immediately available. Through the years, their efforts to get power to the people of Welch have been a challenging yet rewarding endeavor. (Courtesy of the City of Welch.)

COME AND GET IT. Frank Darras is shown here at the lunch counter of Chris Mitro's Capitol Lunch on Railroad Avenue at Howard Street in this photograph from the Huger Collection. Welch residents enjoyed some of the best Greek cooking in West Virginia. (Courtesy of Jay Chapman.)

ALL THE NEWS THAT FITS THE PRINT. A couple of *Welch Daily News* reporters—James Hall, left, and Frank Moreno, right—are shown here seated in front of an unidentified man wearing a suit and tie. *WDN* reporters covered the coalfield beat. (Courtesy of the City of Welch.)

NUMBER PLEASE. By 1958, the Welch Telephone switchboard operators had grown to 20 in number. The company became part of the GTE South system and is now a Frontier Communications system. (Courtesy of Louise Warden.)

HAPPY MOTORING. Ed Shepard's Ford at Coney Island in Welch, shown in this Huger Collection photograph, was a popular place for drivers to find a new car. (Courtesy of Jay Chapman.)

AIR WELCH. The Welch Airport, located on Belcher Mountain about three miles east-southeast of Welch, started out as a Works Progress Administration project in 1934, although the project was not completed at that time. The Welch Moose Lodge pushed for completion of the project in 1946, and W. B. Swope and others built the first hangar at the airport in 1948. Note Starland Drive-In Theater a few hundred yards east of the runway. (Aerial photograph by Mel Grubb.)

A LEAGUE OF THEIR OWN. The Welch Jaycees Little League team shown here was coached by Jack Christian (far left) and Harry Camper (far right). From left to right are (first row) Christian, Michael Vallo, unidentified, Charles Mathena, Ralph Waller-Henrico, unidentified, Victor Nystrum, and Camper; (second row) Mark Winter, Harry Ballard, unidentified, ? Cartwright, and Herman Wilson. The player kneeling is unidentified. (Courtesy of the City of Welch.)

HOOPSTERS. Members of a Welch High School basketball team are shown here in this Huger Collection photograph. From left to right are (seated) H. C. "Kit" Lewis Jr., Jack Farthing, Marvin Woodie, Jack Sizemore, and Joe Orrison; (standing) Philip Brunschwyler, Bobby Marrs, Jim Brown, Donald Dye, and Charles "Bud" Gearhart. (Courtesy of Jay Chapman.)

STEVENS CLINIC IN WINTER. The Stevens Clinic Hospital in Welch, shown in this Huger Collection photograph, was opened in 1930 as a unit of the Bluefield Sanitarium. Dr. W. B. Stevens of Kimball and Dr. Harry G. Camper of Welch worked with doctors Wade St. Clair and R. O. Rogers of Bluefield to open the hospital. The hospital started out as a 100-bed facility but soon expanded to 140 beds. A home for nurses opened in 1948. The hospital closed in 1987, and the building was remodeled and opened as the Stevens Correctional Facility in 2006. (Courtesy of Jay Chapman.)

Four

METROPOLITAN EMERGENCE

COMFORT AND CONVENIENCE. A group of models and actors played the parts of travelers and railroad personnel for promotional material related to the Norfolk and Western Railway's April 28, 1946, launch of the "New Powhatan Arrow" streamlined passenger service from Cincinnati, Ohio, to Norfolk, Virginia, through Welch. (Courtesy of Carlton Viar.)

WELCH. This incredible aerial photograph, taken by David P. Cruise for the *Welch Daily News*, shows the city in 1947, even before Welch reached its peak population of 6,600 people during the 1950s. The city grew around the tree-surrounded knoll where the McDowell County Courthouse stands. Note the World War I Memorial behind the courthouse and the Norfolk and Western passenger station on Howard Street along the railroad tracks. The N&W Railroad mainline

makes a sweeping U-curve through the heart of downtown Welch following the meanderings of Elkhorn Creek where it meets the Tug Fork of the Big Sandy River in the lower central portion of the photograph. The N&W McDowell Street crossing and the Welch Municipal Parking Garage are also dominant features in the photograph. (Courtesy of the West Virginia Room Collection, McDowell County Public Library.)

PARKING FINE. The City of Welch came up with a novel solution to the community's ongoing parking problems by erecting a multi-level parking facility in the heart of the downtown—the first ever municipally owned parking facility in the United States. Mayor B. F. Howard developed the municipal parking garage during his first term as mayor from 1940 through July 1, 1944. He returned to the position in 1950. City council respected Howard's commitments to the city's growth so much that they renamed Railroad Avenue Howard Avenue in his honor. (Courtesy of the West Virginia Room Collection, McDowell County Public Library.)

SET A SPELL. Everybody's Lunch on Railroad Avenue in Welch, shown in this Huger Collection photograph, was a popular meeting place for African American residents of Welch, as well as for people passing through the city on their way to other coalfield destinations. The restaurant enjoyed a great reputation for good food at least as far away as Bluefield. (Courtesy of Jay Chapman.)

POLE WORKER. The unidentified man shown here in this Huger Collection photograph is obviously taking advantage of his high position to enjoy a bird's-eye view of the city. The flagpole is located on Wyoming Street. (Courtesy of Jay Chapman.)

CHANGING TIMES. The downtown section of Welch is constantly changing as can be seen in this 1982 view of the city. The old Welch War Memorial building had already been torn down by the time this aerial photograph by Mel Grubb had been taken. (Courtesy of the West Virginia Room Collection, McDowell County Public Library.)

TOWN MATTERS. This photograph by Jim Christea shows Welch in the 1960s with the old Norfolk and Western passenger station in the foreground and the World War I Memorial building in the center of the photograph. (Courtesy of the City of Welch.)

BLUE BIRD OF HAPPINESS. The unidentified young man shown here in this photograph from the Huger Collection appears to have a desire to examine a bicycle parked near the Blue Bird Lunch on McDowell Street in Welch. (Courtesy of Jay Chapman.)

LIGHT WORK. Welch mayor B. F. Howard is shown here flipping on the switch to illuminate a 1958 streetlight project in Coney Island. Howard was born in 1895 and was a member of the first Welch High School graduating class. He studied law at Washington and Lee University, served in World War I, and began his law practice in Welch in 1922. Shown here at the lighting ceremony are, from left to right, Pat Horne, W. B. Swope, Marvin Probst, Mayor Howard, Ray Wilson, Albert Barley, Meyer Bell, and Joe G. Travis. (Courtesy of the West Virginia Room Collection, McDowell County Public Library.)

To the Dump. This Huger Collection photograph shows a modern solid waste disposal truck owned by the City of Welch. The truck is pictured on Wyoming Street near the *Welch Daily News* building. (Courtesy of Jay Chapman.)

Grocery Shopping. The huge Elkhorn Valley Grocery Company warehouse on Howard Street in Welch, shown here in this photograph from the Huger Collection, provided foodstuffs to Welch and surrounding communities. The Welch Street Department now uses the building. (Courtesy of Jay Chapman.)

VANTAGE POINT. This snow scene from the Huger Collection shows a rooftop view of several buildings in Welch. Floods during the first decade of the 21st century prompted the removal of several older structures. (Courtesy of Jay Chapman.)

SCENE OF DESTRUCTION. An unidentified police officer appears to be sorting through the brick debris associated with a fire on McDowell Street that destroyed several buildings, including a jewelry store and a shoe repair shop, as shown in this photograph from the Huger Collection. (Courtesy of Jay Chapman.)

ON THE RIGHT TRACK. A group of men is shown in this photograph from the Huger Collection lining up to enter the Vick Building at a time when the Norfolk and Western Railway went through the heart of downtown Welch. (Courtesy of Jay Chapman.)

TOW TO TANGO. Several Welch residents speculated as to who the tow truck driver in this Huger Collection photograph is, but they ultimately could not agree. Center Auto Sales was a mainstay business in downtown Welch for many years. (Courtesy of Jay Chapman.)

FOR THE KIDS. Santa Claus is shown here holding an unidentified, but still excited, young girl in his arms. For many years, the Welch Lions Club sponsored a visit by Santa to talk with children in advance of his big day. (Courtesy of the City of Welch.)

IN THE CATBIRD SEAT. The unidentified Norfolk and Western Railway employee shown in this photograph from the Huger Collection was responsible for raising and lowering the crossing gates at the McDowell Street grade crossing. (Courtesy of Jay Chapman.)

KIDS' STUFF. Children from throughout McDowell County marched down McDowell Street in Welch in the Centennial Kiddies' Day Parade, one of the many activities associated with the 1958 centennial celebration. (Courtesy of the City of Welch.)

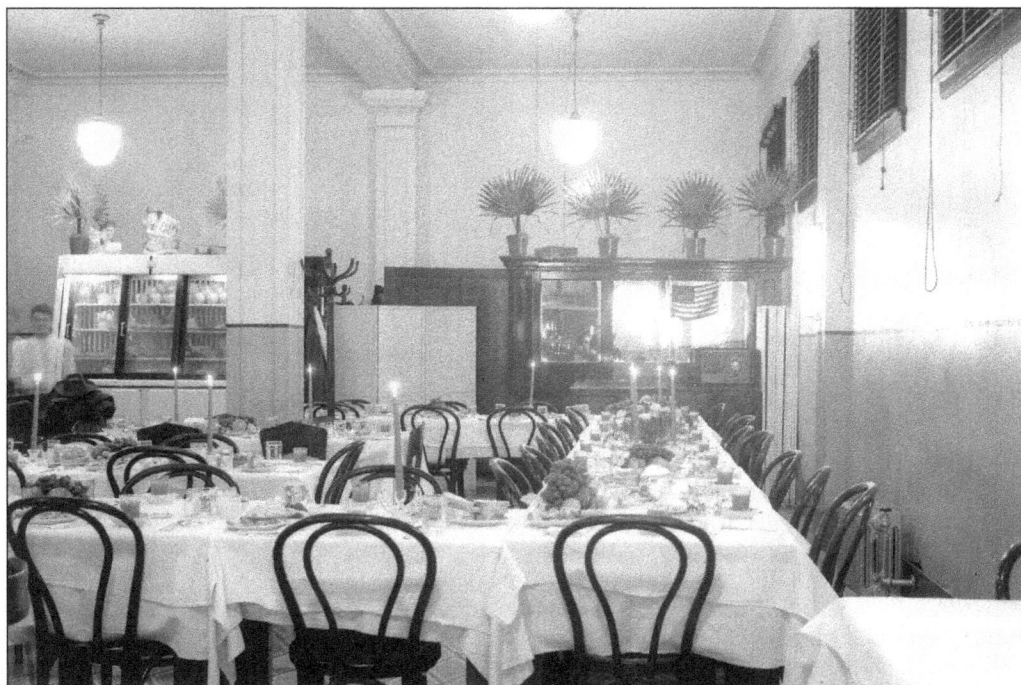

FINE DINING. The Central Café of the Carter Hotel in Welch looks to be ready to host a formal banquet in this photograph from the Huger Collection. (Courtesy of Jay Chapman.)

ROOM FOR YOU. An unidentified desk clerk appears to be ready to check guests into the old Carter Hotel in this Huger Collection photograph. (Courtesy of Jay Chapman.)

PRIDE OF LIONS. Members of the Welch Lions Club are shown meeting with W. R. "Pete" Cook of Bluefield. From left to right are (seated) Seldon Albert, Dick Rutt, Dr. A. J. Villani, Pete Cook, and Joe Romano; (standing) ? Randolph, Buddy Hunt, unidentified, Louis Pais, Chester Matney, C. P. Settle, Jimmy Johns, and Sam Sidote. (Courtesy of the City of Welch.)

OLD SCHOOL MEETING. Mrs. Frances F. Long of Welch is shown here meeting with Dean R. L. Stump (left) of West Virginia University and WVU president H. B. Heflin. Mrs. Long served as supervisor of special education in McDowell County from 1959 until her retirement in 1969. (Courtesy of the City of Welch.)

NICE DAY FOR A WALK. Two unidentified young ladies are shown here in this photograph from the Huger Collection walking on a sidewalk in Welch. The steep terrain surrounding the city doesn't prevent Welch from being a community that can be enjoyed by foot. (Courtesy of Jay Chapman.)

ARMOR EMPLOYEES. The group of Armor Meats employees shown in this photograph includes Charlie P. Cornett, seated at the far right; Charles Fletcher, standing at the far left; and Tom Calloway, standing at the far right, who managed the Armor branch office in Northfork. (Courtesy of Jay Chapman.)

RUBBER CHICKEN CIRCUIT. H. C. "Kit" Lewis Jr., shown here seated at the end of the table in the foreground, couldn't recall the reason for the dinner but said the fried chicken was good. The dinner was held in the old Welch fire hall. (Courtesy of the City of Welch.)

COMMUNITY LEADERS. O. J. Hunter, shown here seated at the far left, was the father of the great playwright Kermit Hunter, who penned several outdoor, historical dramas. From left to right are (seated) Hunter, Bob Johnson of G. B. Construction Company, and unidentified; (standing) two unidentified, Charlie Martin, and John Lane. (Courtesy of Jim Fields.)

WELCH LAW. Leon P. Miller was a partner in the Capehart and Miller law firm in Welch; served as assistant McDowell County prosecutor; was elected to Welch city council in 1944; was elected McDowell County circuit court judge in 1948; and was appointed by Pres. Dwight D. Eisenhower in 1954 as U.S. attorney for the U.S. Virgin Islands. (Courtesy of the West Virginia Room Collection, McDowell County Public Library.)

OUTDOORSMAN. Kermit Hounton Hunter was born in McDowell County on October 2, 1910, and grew up in Welch. He graduated from Ohio State in 1931, and after a stint as a colonel in the U.S. Army during World War II, he worked as business manager for the North Carolina Symphony. Hunter is best known for the 40 outdoor dramas he wrote, including *Unto these Hills*, *The Road Home*, and *Honey in the Rock*. Hunter died on April 11, 2001. (Courtesy of Theatre West Virginia.)

OLDER SCHOOL. This photograph from the Huger Collection shows students from an unidentified Welch school seated in a classroom and ready to learn. (Courtesy of Jay Chapman.)

NEW BALL GAME. Paul Jones, right, is shown here at the dedication of the Little League Park in Welch. Jones donated the park to the city. Jones is shaking hands with Larry Smithburger, who was league president at the time of the donation. (Courtesy of the City of Welch.)

HOPE FLOATS. Johnny Villani, the "voice" of WELC Radio at the time, is shown standing on the station's float making some last-minute adjustments to the WELC float before traversing Welch during the annual Veterans Day Parade. The unidentified young lady at the front of the float worked in the station office, and the young man working on the loud speaker is not identified. (Courtesy of Sam Sidote.)

BARGAIN HUNTERS. Welch mayor B. F. Howard and Hobart Payne are shown here rolling up McDowell Street in a 1921 Model T Ford to lead the 1955 Old Fashioned Bargain Day Parade. Note the grade crossing and the crossing gates in the right of the photograph. (Courtesy of the West Virginia Room Collection, McDowell County Public Library.)

MAN IN MOTION. Welch mayor B. F. Howard appears to be enjoying the ride as he tools this old Model T Ford up McDowell Street in the May 1958 McDowell County Centennial Parade. While many spectators dressed in olden-day fashions, facial hair—real or faux—was the order of the day for the men of the county. (Courtesy of the West Virginia Room Collection, McDowell County Public Library.)

FASHION PLATES. Several of Welch's leading ladies got all gussied up for the Beta Sigma Phi Hobo Party on November 18, 1949. From left to right are (first row) A. Gray, Frances Holiway, Mary R. Christie, Mary Marshall, Betty J. Callaway, Herma Barber, Millie Edwards, and Elizabeth Ricci; (second row, not in order) Hattie Jane Evans, Louise Belcher, Joyce Callaway, Rosemary Brunschwyler, Barbara Sheldon, Estelle Geetz, Dorothy Bowen, Ann Harvey, Catherine Albert, and unidentified; (third row) Helen Dawson, Mary Rogers, Freda Booth, Jean Mayhew, Virginia Jervis, June Caudill, Virginia Reynolds, Sadie Belcher, Jerry Scholl, Virginia Ferris, and Ann Martin; (fourth row) Mary Dalton, Juanita Lawrence, Mary Fanning, Theodore Albert, Mary Stafford, Myrtle Roberts, Dent Todd, and Beulah Gianato. (Courtesy of the City of Welch.)

STAR OF THE SHOW. McDowell County officials went all out for the formal coronation of McDowell County Centennial queen Dorothy Miller in a huge ceremony staged at the Welch High School Maroon Wave Stadium in 1958. Former West Virginia governor Cecil Underwood crowned Miller, and the elaborate set was also used to stage the grand finale of the centennial play, *Our Changing Hills*, authored by Joseph T. Newlin. (Courtesy of the West Virginia Room Collection, McDowell County Public Library.)

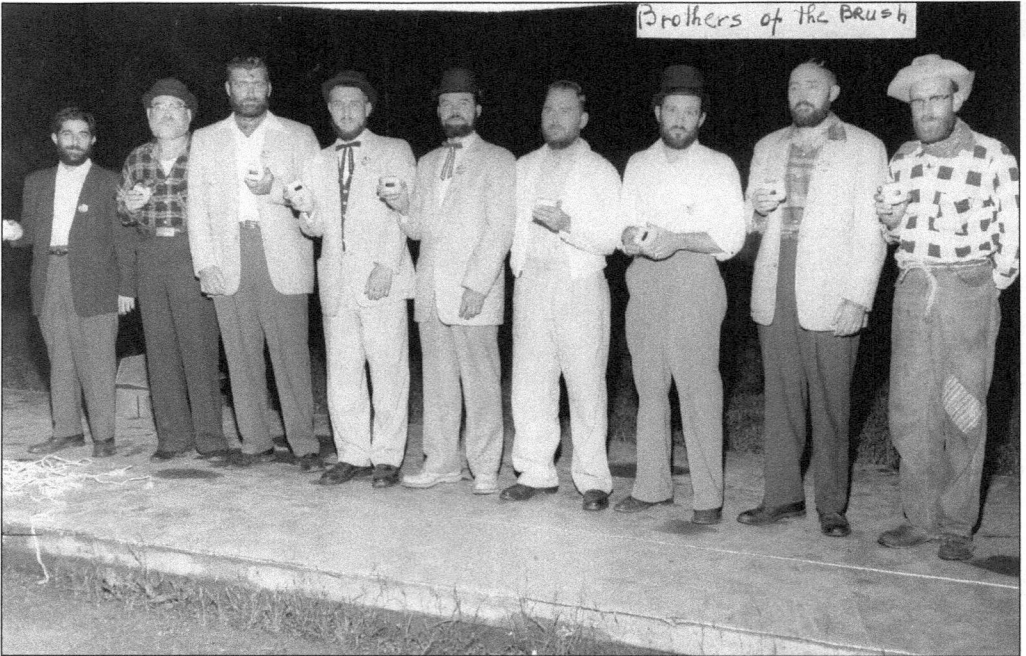

Brothers of the Brush

BROTHERS OF THE BRUSH. One of the most memorable elements of the McDowell County Centennial was the "Brothers of the Brush" facial hair–growing contest. This photograph shows the brothers after about three months of growth. From left to right are Tony Romeo, unidentified, B. Fanning, unidentified, John Lane David, unidentified, Walter Wagers, unidentified, and Bernard Groseclose. (Courtesy of the City of Welch.)

THE KINDEST CUT. The Brothers of the Brush are shown here after shaving. Tony Romeo (far left) recalls winning a Remington razor for having the best beard. Other winners included Gail Walker, who sported the best muttonchops; James B. Manning, who had the best van dyke; Charles Pruitt, who had the best chin whiskers; and Ralph Byrd, who had the best full beard. (Courtesy of the City of Welch.)

REGAL MAROON WAVE. Dorothy Mitchell traveled in style during the McDowell County Centennial Parade on top of this lovely float created by WELC Radio. The Centennial Parade got underway at 5:30 p.m., on May 12, 1958, with former-governor Cecil Underwood serving as grand marshal. (Courtesy of Sam Sidote.)

LOOKING GOOD. The Centennial Belles and a few of the Brothers of the Brush gathered in front of Norfolk and Western locomotive No. 475 for this promotional photograph by Woody's Studio. The centennial celebration was a weeklong festival of the Free State of McDowell. Jerry Fralick thinks the man on the far right of this photograph is his father, John C. Fralick. (Courtesy of Louise Warden.)

Five

THE TEST OF TIME

KEEPING IT CLEAN. The Welch Chamber of Commerce organized a "Keep Welch Clean" drive and encouraged citizens to get involved in keeping the city beautiful. This photograph was taken from the grade-crossing observation booth. (Courtesy of the City of Welch.)

GIVE 'EM SWELL, HARRY. Former U.S. president Harry S. Truman (right) shown here in 1957 with D. C. Bradbury, founder and owner of WELC Radio, was instrumental in the resurrection of Welch's annual Veterans Day Parade. At the invitation of Sam Solins, Truman served as the keynote speaker of a Veterans Day Parade in Welch on November 11, 1941, while he was serving as U.S. senator from Missouri. The parade tradition originated in 1919, when Hanford MacNider, national commander of the American Legion, was keynote speaker. The 1920 speaker was Col. Theodore Roosevelt, assistant secretary of the army. Truman returned to the Welch Veterans Day Parade in 1957 after serving as president. WELC Radio began broadcasting in 1950. (Courtesy of Sam Sidote.)

COALFIELD CAMELOT. Pres. John F. Kennedy visited Welch in late April and early May 1960 when he was campaigning for the Democratic nomination for president. Huge crowds turned out for Kennedy wherever he stopped. Eight years later in 1968, his brother, Bobby Kennedy, retraced John's campaign trail through West Virginia and received a cold welcome because of his opposition to the Vietnam War. W. B. Swope, mayor of Welch at the time of Bobby Kennedy's visit and a staunch Republican, made the younger Kennedy feel welcome and maintained frequent communications with him right up until his assassination later that summer in California. (Courtesy of the City of Welch.)

LBJ IN THE FREE STATE. Vice Pres. Lyndon Johnson served as keynote speaker at the Welch Veterans Day Parade on November 11, 1963—just 12 days before an assassin would kill Pres. John F. Kennedy and make Johnson the most powerful leader of the free world. An unidentified Secret Service man keeps a close watch on the crowd in Welch, estimated at 10,000, while Johnson rides with L. Oblinger (center) and Sam Solins, chairman of the McDowell County Post No. 8 American Legion speakers committee. (Courtesy of the City of Welch.)

GREAT SOCIETY. Pres. Lyndon Johnson appears humbled as Thornton Berry leads the applause during a speaking engagement in November 1963 in Welch. Berry was a notable Welch lawyer with a distinguished navy career and was one of three men from Welch who were promoted to lieutenant commander, U.S. Navy Reserves, in 1946. Berry was elected to the West Virginia State Supreme Court of Appeals in 1958 and became chief justice in 1973. (Courtesy of the City of Welch.)

ON TOUR. Hubert H. Humphrey Jr. and his wife, Muriel (Buck) Humphrey, are shown strolling through the streets of downtown Welch on a tour guided by Sam Solins. Humphrey was serving as U.S. senator from Minnesota in 1960 and was in a tough primary race with John F. Kennedy during the May 1960 primary in West Virginia. (Courtesy of the City of Welch.)

TALKING POLITICS. Sam Solins (right) is shown here visiting with West Virginia governor Hulett Smith. Welch has been a political hotbed for years and a Democratic stronghold since the Pres. Franklin D. Roosevelt era. (Courtesy of the City of Welch.)

LOVE A PARADE. The people of Welch traditionally turn out in huge numbers to watch parades down McDowell Street, including this event billed as the "Lewis Day Parade" in the Welch photograph archives. Members of the H. C. Lewis family have been among the city's most ardent supporters. (Courtesy of the City of Welch.)

ROCKY ROAD. New York governor Nelson A. Rockefeller (front, second from left) is shown touring the streets of Welch, most likely in 1964 during his unsuccessful campaign for the Republican party presidential nomination. The man on the far left is unidentified, but the others, from left to right, are Rockefeller, Jim Ballard, Jack Beamer, former West Virginia governor Cecil Underwood, and Lt. Col. Wade Hampton Ballard II (retired U.S. Air Force) tipping his hat. Lieutenant Colonel Ballard was head of the McDowell County Republican Club at the time. (Courtesy of the City of Welch.)

PLAY BALL. The 1941 Welch Miners of the Mountain State League are shown here posing for a team picture in this photograph from the Huger Collection. While organized professional baseball in the coalfields was common throughout the 20th century when many coal companies fielded professional teams, the only major league affiliation was the Class D, Mountain State League from 1937 through the end of the 1941 season. The six-team league included the Beckley Bengals, the Huntington Booster Bees, the Logan Indians, the Williamson Colts, the Bluefield Blue Grays, and the Welch Miners. The league's most famous alumnus was Stan Musial, who pitched for Williamson in the 1938 and 1939 seasons until he developed a sore arm and his manager converted him to a hitter. Raymond "Lefty" Guard of Princeton said the batboy (reclining front) was Vernon Suiter, but he couldn't recall the name of the bus driver not in uniform at the back of the group. "We called him Bussy," Guard said. The players are, from left to right (first row) Don Manno, manager; Cookie Nickles, catcher; Rick Jackson; Bob Brady; unidentified; and Vernon Bickford; (second row) Hans Hines, Larry King, Lefty Guard (with hands on shoulders of Rick Jackson), Sammy House, Zeb Sinder, and Carlos Rátliff. (Courtesy of Jay Chapman.)

PITCHMAN. Welch mayor W. B. Swope looks to be making a pitch from the cheap seats. Swope was active in all aspects of life in Welch and, in spite of his Republican Party affiliation, kept getting reelected year after year in largely Democratic Welch. (Courtesy of the City of Welch.)

MUSTANG. Ronnie Coe and his son, Mike, are shown here with the green 1965 Ford Mustang that Coe won in a drawing August 27, 1965, at the Starland Theatre. Businesses throughout Welch sold chances on the popular Mustang, and Coe, who had a coal trucking business in Welch at the time, took his change in tickets when he traded at those businesses. Although he still has the ticket that won him the car, he laments the fact that he doesn't have the Mustang. (Courtesy of Ronnie Coe.)

MARCH MADNESS. Coach Frank Moreno (fourth from left, short-sleeve shirt, touching trophy) is shown here with the county champion Welch High School Maroon Wave basketball team in this March 6, 1971, photograph. The coaches to the far right of the photograph are Ed Mosko (wearing glasses) and Victor Nystrom. Coach Moreno was a star athlete at Welch High School and became basketball coach in 1964, added the football coaching chores in 1969, and coached until 1977. (Courtesy of the City of Welch.)

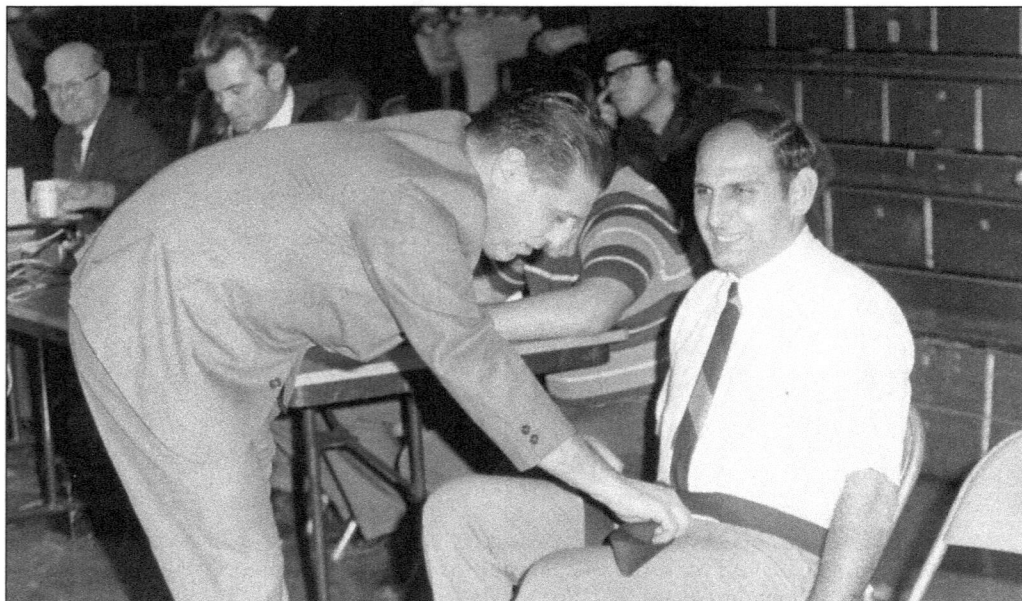

SAFETY RESTRAINT. Sam Romeo, longtime Welch High School principal, is shown here strapping WHS boys' basketball coach Frank Moreno in his chair after a 1971 ruling requiring coaches to remain seated during games. Romeo was named WHS principal in 1969 after 19 years as an educator in McDowell County Schools. (Courtesy of the City of Welch.)

THE GREAT MO. Maurice "Tree" Robinson, an All-State basketball player at Welch High School who later starred as a forward on the West Virginia University basketball team, is one of the greatest basketball players from Welch. The Morgantown Touchdown Club selected Robinson "Basketball Player of the Year" in 1974. During his junior year at West Virginia, he averaged 19.9 points per game and was named first team All-Eastern 8. He was drafted by the Atlanta Hawks but did not play in the NBA. (Courtesy of the City of Welch.)

DUO. Ray Blevins (left) and Jimmy Davis are shown here during a live performance on WELC Radio. Through the years, WELC has been a launching pad for the careers of many famous performers. Perhaps the most famous WELC alumnus was Mel Street, who sang on the station when he was 13 years old. Street was born in Buchanan County, Virginia, but his family moved to the Welch area when he was young. WELC was founded in 1949 by Sam Sidote, D. C. Bradbury, and H.R. King and went on the air on August 19, 1950. (Courtesy of Cecil Surratt.)

COWBOY ACT. Coalwood native Cecil Surratt, shown here at age 18, in this photograph dated October 23, 1944, played his first radio gig on Welch station WBRW when he was just 14 years old—the year the station went on the air. WBRW's call letters came from the first initial of the last name of the station founders, John W. Blakely, L. E. Rogers, and J. Read Werness. WBRW ceased broadcasting on April 30, 1955, and sold its assets to WELC Radio. (Courtesy of Cecil Surratt.)

YOUNG PEOPLE FROM MCDOWELL. U.S. Senators Jennings Randolph and Robert C. Byrd (far left, standing) are shown here with this group of young people from McDowell County. The Welch photograph archives did not have additional information concerning the photograph, but it is significant because of the longtime support of the two senators. (Courtesy of the City of Welch.)

COOL POOL. Young people in Welch know how to beat the heat by splashing around the city-owned Linkous Park swimming pool as shown here in this July 25, 1985, photograph. (Courtesy of the City of Welch.)

FAMOUS POOL. The Linkous Park Pool, shown here in the 1970s, is a famous city landmark thanks to a well-known photograph by O. Winston Link of a 1950s vintage night view of the pool with a Norfolk and Western steam locomotive in the background. (Courtesy of the City of Welch.)

GOOD SCOUTS. Youth activities were always a big part of life in Welch, and these young Boy Scouts are all smiles. From left to right are Bruce Lewis, Wayne Sorah, Richard Hanson, Bruce Martin, Dick Gale, and Scoutmaster Victor Nystrom. (Courtesy of the City of Welch.)

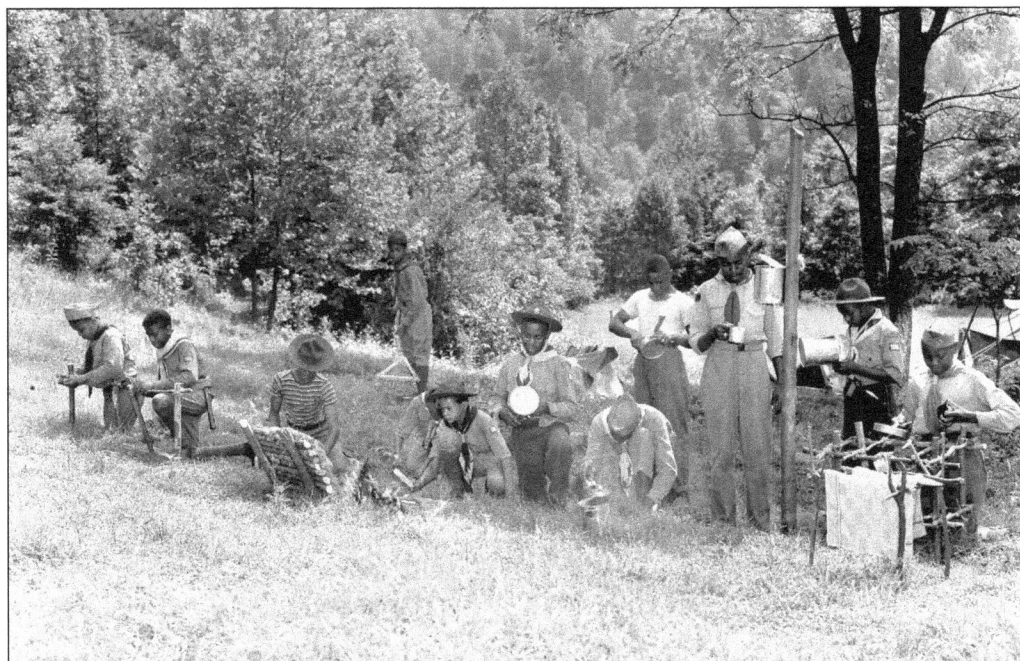

SCOUTING ADVENTURE. Scouting in McDowell County dates back to 1925. Young people, like the African American troop shown in this photograph from the Huger Collection, enjoyed outdoor activities as well as other character-building endeavors. (Courtesy of Jay Chapman.)

GIVE TO THE CAUSE. Members of the Welch Lions Club are shown here as they launch a fundraising effort for the March of Dimes. From left to right are Mario Delcont, Tony Romeo, ? Cowan, and Granville "Rocky" Sexton. (Courtesy of the City of Welch.)

HELPING HAND. Welch's active William E. Eubank Voiture 1171 of the 40&8 veterans group has been active on a broad civic front for several years, including a "King-for-a-Day" program where the 40&8 sponsored disabled children for a trip to Charleston and a special outing just for them. While the child holding the balloons and the man in the 40&8 smock are unidentified, Gloria Chewning is pictured at the far left, Gwendolyn Johnson from Kimball is in the foreground, and T. J. Scott is behind Johnson. (Courtesy of the City of Welch.)

THE AMAZING ROLLO. Veteran *Welch Daily News* newsman Rollo Taylor (left) is shown here demonstrating the operation of an unidentified apparatus to *WDN* general manager W. R. "Will" Keyser, a Tyler County native who came to Welch to found the newspaper in 1923 at the urging of H. C. Ogden, publisher of the *Wheeling Intelligencer*. Roland "Rollo" Taylor, a graduate of the University of North Carolina School of Journalism, was the paper's star reporter for many years before being appointed general manager in 1963. (Courtesy of the West Virginia Room Collection, McDowell County Public Library.)

THE GANG'S ALL HERE. W. R. "Will" Keyser (light suit, wearing glasses at front table) sponsored a dinner for employees of the *Welch Daily News*. The newspaper's first edition was published on December 3, 1923. In 1927, the newspaper moved to its present home in a three-story building on Wyoming Street. In 1958, the *WDN* had a circulation of about 15,000 newspapers delivered by some 250 carriers each afternoon. The newspaper changed from publishing six to five days a week in the 1990s and down to three days per week in the early 21st century. In 2003, the newspaper's circulation was 5,500. (Courtesy of the City of Welch.)

HONORED TO SERVE. Members of the Welch Fire Department are shown posing by their equipment in this photograph. Jerry Rotenberry is the fifth man from the left in the second row, but the other firefighters were not identified in the Welch City Hall Archives. D. L. Salisbury was appointed fire chief in 1954, and in 1958, he supplied information to the *Welch Daily News* that the department was organized *c.* 1900 and that in the early days, volunteers were alerted to fires by shouts and guns being fired in the air. The city formally organized the Welch Volunteer Fire Department in August 1921. The department grew steadily through the years, and after some years of having paid firefighters, the department returned to volunteer status in the late 1980s. (Courtesy of the City of Welch.)

FOR ART'S SAKE. Well-known Welch photographers Ruth and Ron Justice operated Ron J. Studio on McDowell Street. Mr. and Mrs. Justice captured images of countless thousands of Welch students and brides through the years. Ron Justice joined Woody's Studio in 1956, became manager of the studio when Woody's moved to Bristol, Tennessee, in 1960, and later bought Woody's. (Courtesy of the City of Welch.)

McDOWELL STREET FIRE. The old DeMario's Furniture warehouse was badly damaged as shown in this undated Huger Collection photograph. The Rucci and Sons grocery and pastry shop, owned by Nick and Ester Rucci, is shown in the left of this photograph. (Courtesy of Jay Chapman.)

NOT HORSING AROUND. H. C. "Kit" Lewis Jr. is shown here aboard a donkey getting ready to participate in a charity sporting contest. It is fitting that Lewis is riding a donkey because he has been active in Democratic Party politics since his youth, and at the time this book was written, he was serving as chairman of the McDowell County Democratic Party. (Courtesy of the City of Welch.)

SCHOOL HOUSE ROCKS. Students of Hazel Olinger's class at Welch Elementary School are shown here eager to learn. Olinger taught school at Welch Elementary for 44 years. In 1925, she and her husband, Bill, owned and operated a popular gas station on Wyoming Street where the courthouse annex is now located. (Courtesy of the City of Welch.)

SOMETHING FOR CHILDREN. The Welch Lions Club hosted an annual Christmas party for children in the area. This event was held in 1952. (Courtesy of the City of Welch.)

Snow Coated. The Russell Burge home, shown in this photograph from the Huger Collection in a winter scene, was formerly the home of veteran *Welch Daily News* reporter Rollo Taylor. (Courtesy of Jay Chapman.)

Welch in the Spring. The Mark Jones home shown in this photograph from the Huger Collection is located in Welch's posh Southwood Addition. (Courtesy of Jay Chapman.)

DEMOCRATIC HEADQUARTERS. Members of the McDowell County Democratic Women's Committee are shown here at party headquarters on Elkhorn Street. From left to right are Mrs. Cecil Phillips, Mrs. George Lockhart, Miss Doris Phillips, Mrs. Dave White, and Committee Chairperson Mrs. Charles (Lois) Conner. (Courtesy of the City of Welch.)

MARCH GLADNESS. Pat Marino is shown here receiving a contribution to the March of Dimes collected by Welch High School students. From left to right are Mrs. ? Ross, Terri Lewis, Debbie Goode, ? Groseclose, Pat Marino, and Mark Chatfield. (Courtesy of the City of Welch.)

NEEDS REPAIR. The Welch municipal parking garage shown in this photograph dated January 29, 1985, was in need of repairs. The city undertook a major refurbishment of the historic facility and restored it to good condition. (Courtesy of the City of Welch.)

HILLSIDE HOMES. Residences on Grandview Street in Welch demonstrate the challenge builders faced in trying to erect housing on the steep hillsides surrounding the community. (Courtesy of the City of Welch.)

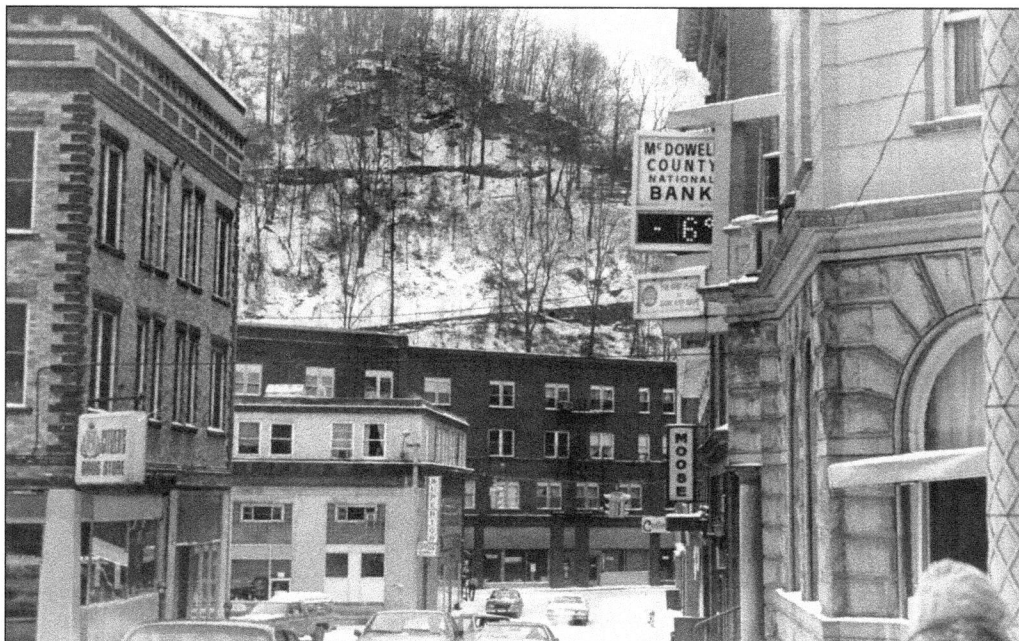

IT CAN GET COLD IN WELCH. The thermometer outside the McDowell County National Bank shows outside air temperature of minus-six degrees. In spite of the fact that Welch is south of Richmond, Virginia, winters are traditionally prone to a cold snap or two. (Courtesy of the City of Welch.)

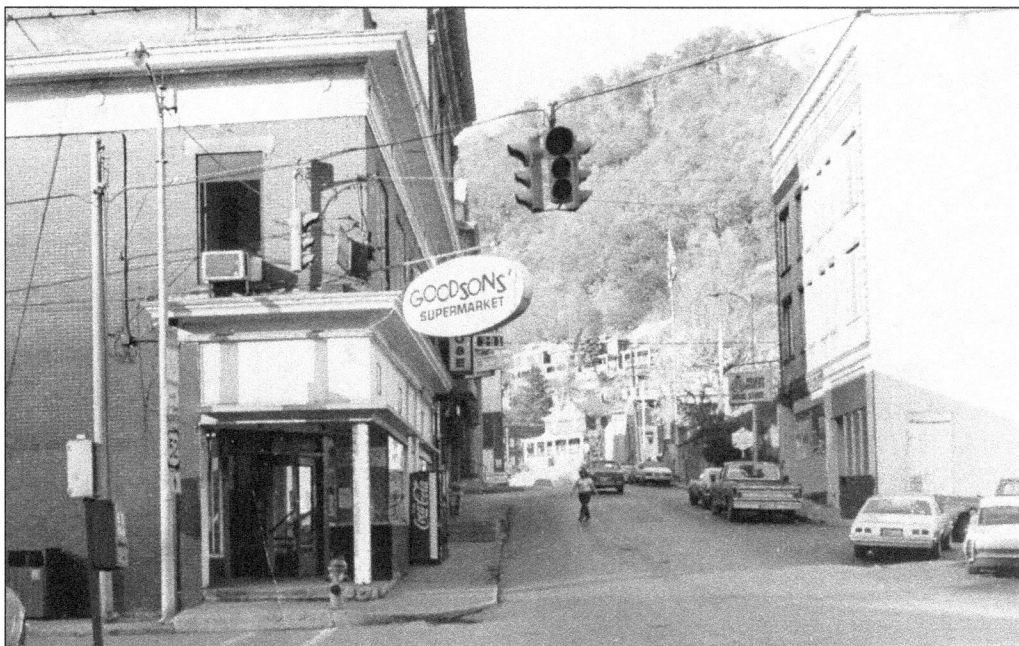

FOOD BASKET. The Goodson family has been supplying food to the citizens of Welch and surrounding communities since the early years of the 20th century. The old Goodsons' Super Market was located on the corning of Wyoming and Howard Streets. (Courtesy of the City of Welch.)

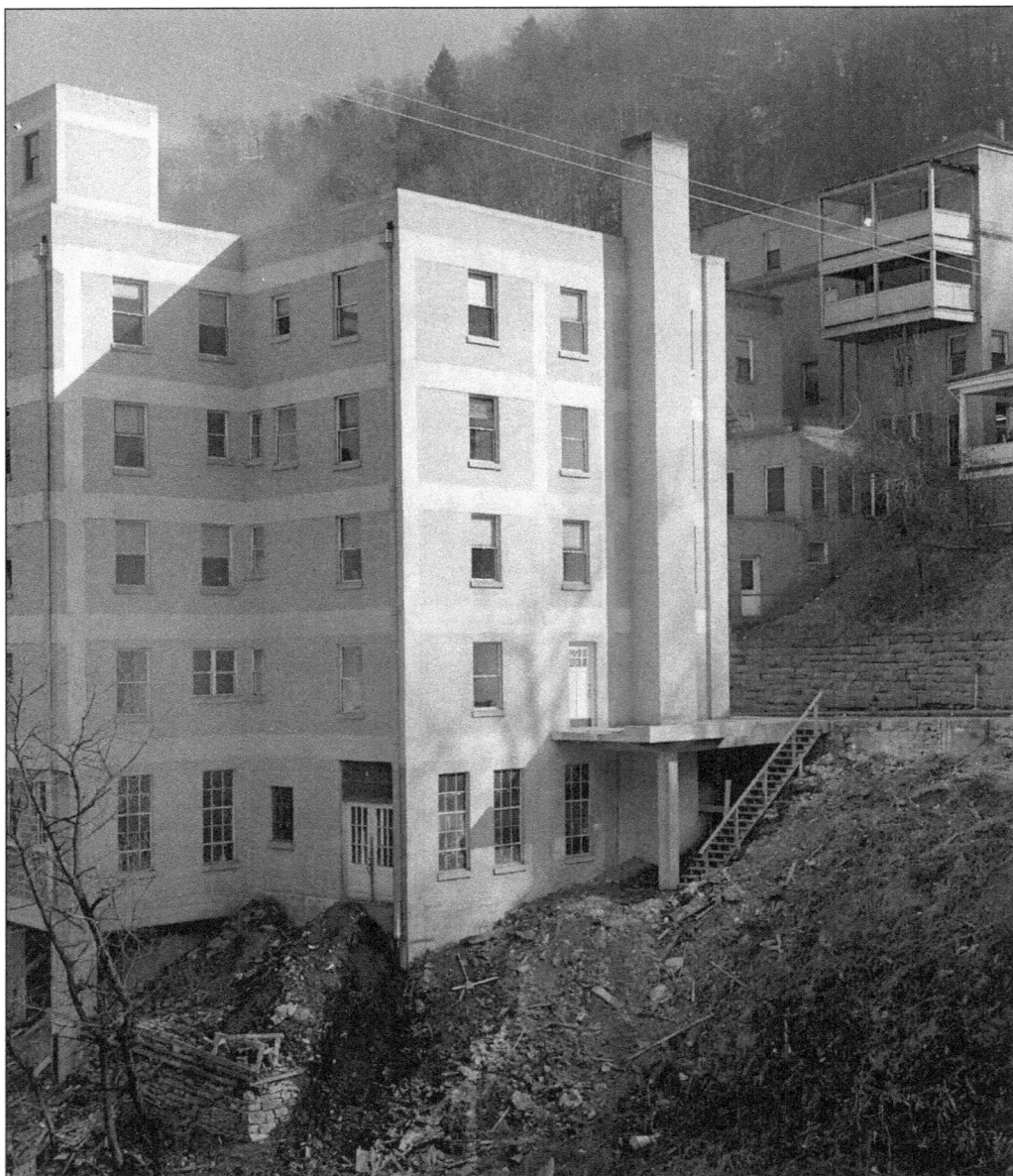

GRACE BY THE RIVER. The old Grace Hospital is shown from the Tug Fork of the Big Sandy River side in this photograph from the Huger Collection. Grace Hospital was chartered in 1923 and spread out on both sides of Virginia Avenue as it grew from 35 beds in the beginning to 163 beds in the late 1950s. Thomas H. S. Curd and Dr. Charles F. Hicks founded the hospital, with Dr. G. L. Straub as chief surgeon and Dr. E. Vermillion on the medical staff. Hicks died in 1931, and Dr. Charles B. Chapman joined the staff after he completed a fellowship at the Mayo Clinic. When coal was king, coal companies provided health care benefits to employees through what was known as a "list practice," similar to the modern Health Maintenance Organization or HMO programs, but Grace was not in the list mix. Grace Hospital helped organize the Associated Hospitals Inc., which provided services to non-coal industry workers. That plan grew into Blue Cross/Blue Shield. (Courtesy of Jay Chapman.)

Six

WELCH RENAISSANCE

ROUND AND ROUND SHE GOES. Charlie Hall and his partner, "Mickey" (center, foreground), of the Tug Twirlers square dancers are shown here during a street fair organized by the Welch Chamber of Commerce. In spite of economic challenges related to the cyclical nature of the coal industry, people in Welch still know how to have a good time. (Courtesy of the City of Welch.)

SALES AND ADVENTURES. Merchants of Welch took to the streets for this citywide sidewalk sale on McDowell Street sometime during the 1980s. (Courtesy of the City of Welch.)

FELLOWSHIP AND POLITICS. The annual Welch 40&8 Oyster Dinner, shown here at the National Guard Armory on Stewart Street, traditionally draws hundreds of guests. The event is usually held about two weeks before the West Virginia state primary election, and on election years, it usually brings out a huge crowd. The event has been moved to Mount View High School in recent years. (Courtesy of the City of Welch.)

LEGION LEADS THE WAY. The McDowell County Post No. 8 of the American Legion has enjoyed a near legendary reputation of supporting area veterans. World War I veterans established the post in May 1920, days after the national organization was founded. McDowell Post 8 hosted the state legion convention in 1926 and started sponsoring Veterans Day parades in Welch in 1919. (Courtesy of the City of Welch.)

ON THE AIR. Donnie Turner, son of cable television pioneer Bill Turner, is shown here broadcasting the news from the Welch Antenna Company's Studio 5, which started broadcasting in September 1981. Bill Turner was among the first to recognize the potential for cable television and laid the foundation for a national company known as Turner Vision based on the early lessons he learned while providing television programming to people in Welch. Donnie Turner served on city council in Welch for a time. (Courtesy of the City of Welch.)

Lacy Wright

ON THE WRIGHT TRACK. State senator Lacy Wright Jr., is shown here in a campaign photograph with several of his neighbors standing behind him. Wright was born in Bradshaw in 1946 and has enjoyed a diverse business and political career in the region. He was first elected to the West Virginia House of Delegates in 1974, and by 1984, he was serving in the state Senate. Wright returned to the House but stepped aside after redistricting claimed one of Welch's seats in the House. He maintains a law practice based in the old First National Bank Building on McDowell Street. (Courtesy of the City of Welch.)

TRACK GIANT. Garnett Edwards Jr., of the Welch suburb of Havaco, became one of the greatest track athletes the state has ever known. After being educated in the Welch public schools, Edwards starred on the West Virginia University track team from 1977 to 1980. He finished second in the 60-meter indoor hurdles at the 1979 NCAA Championships and set seven school records during his collegiate career—including four that still stand: the 55-meter hurdles (7.09), the 110 high hurdles (13.44), the 400 hurdles, (51.77) and the indoor long jump (25 feet, 1.25 inches). His 10.25-second time in the 100-meter dash is second only to Olympic gold medalist James Jett. Edwards was an alternate on the 1980 U.S. Olympic team that did not compete due to the U.S. boycott of the Moscow Olympics because of the Russian presence in Afghanistan. His father, Garnett Edwards Sr., played professional baseball for the Black Welch Miners. (Courtesy of Garnett Edwards.)

113

TRUCK CAPITAL OF WEST VIRGINIA. The City of Welch, the Welch Chamber of Commerce, and the McDowell County Economic Development Authority (EDA) recognized the importance of coal trucking to the county and organized a salute to coal truckers on June 24, 2001. (Photograph by Rev. Tim Hairston.)

TRUCKERS HONORED. Coal truckers from throughout the region parked their trucks along McDowell Street for judging by the committee that organized the Salute to Coal Truck Drivers. (Photograph by Rev. Tim Hairston.)

CHROME AND POLISH. In order for the local coal industry to survive, the operators of several small mines started hauling the coal they mined to preparation plants that cleaned the coal of several mines to prepare it for market. Almost overnight, the importance of coal trucking emerged and became a controversial topic statewide. (Photograph by Rev. Tim Hairston.)

PARADE OF TRUCKS. The nighttime parade of coal trucks through Welch served as the concluding event of the daylong Salute to Coal Truck Drivers in 2001. Jack Caffrey of the EDA and Welch mayor Martha Moore organized the event, but the entire community got behind the unique celebration. (Photograph by Rev. Tim Hairston.)

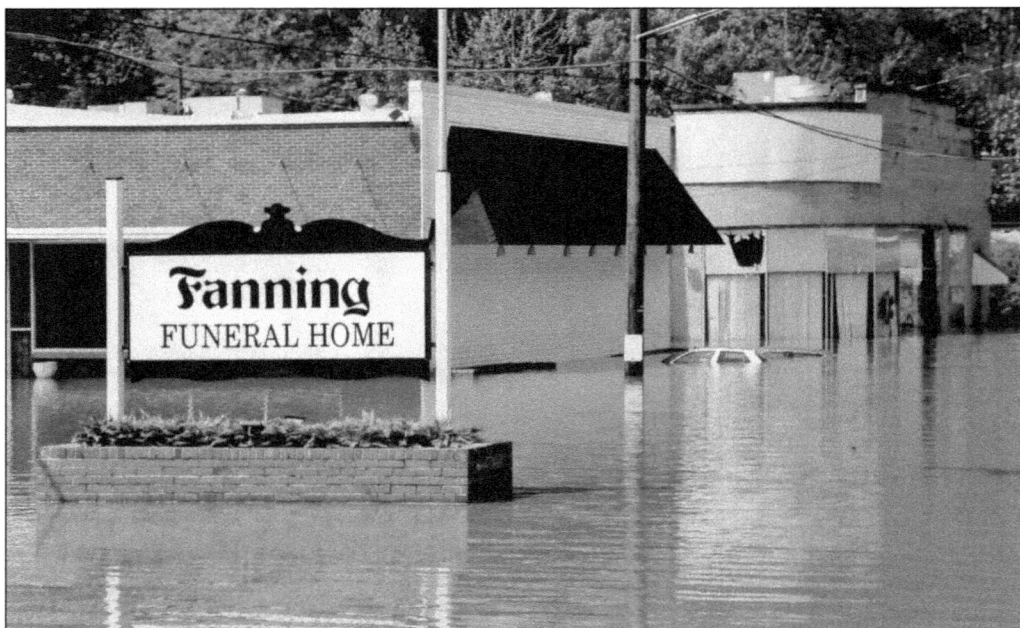

HIGH WATER MARK. Just a few days after Welch was looking its best for the truck parade, a flood struck the city on July 8, 2001. That flood was followed 10 months later by another flood (shown here), which struck on May 2, 2002. The one-two punch was hard to deal with, as witnessed by this photograph of Fanning Funeral Home in Coney Island. (Photograph by Rev. Tim Hairston.)

THE TUG FORK RAN BLACK. As if the flooding wasn't bad enough on May 2, 2002, a coal sludge impoundment in Gary Hollow failed and dumped black water into the Tug Fork of the Big Sandy River, as can be seen in this photograph at Coney Island. (Photograph by the author.)

FLOOD DEBRIS. Lower McDowell Street at the Norfolk Southern underpass was transformed into a quagmire from the flood debris dumped onto the street during the May 2, 2002, flood. Water gathered in both sides of the underpass and made the street impassable to vehicles and trucks. The situation was so bad that only amphibious vehicles could cross. (Photograph by Rev. Tim Hairston.)

MUD RIVER. The banks of the Tug Fork of the Big Sandy River totally covered McDowell Street in the May 2, 2002, flood and pushed back up Wyoming Street, as can be seen here. (Photograph by Rev. Tim Hairston.)

NO PARKING. The heart of Welch was inundated by several feet of floodwater on May 2, 2002. Many of the buildings on McDowell Street could not bounce back after this flood and had to be razed. (Photograph by Evonda Archer.)

HOSPITALIZED. Welch Community Hospital was hard hit by the floodwaters on May 2, 2002. A vehicle on Stewart Street appears bogged down, and a big dump truck on McDowell Street looks to have stopped in its tracks. (Photograph by Rev. Tim Hairston.)

MUD CITY. The Welch Community Hospital emergency room was on high ground and did not get swamped out in the May 2, 2002, flood. The facility continued to provide care through the crisis despite interruptions in communications and utility services during the flood and for some time afterward. (Photograph by Rev. Tim Hairston.)

DOWN BUT NOT OUT. As they have done for 100-plus years, the people of Welch started digging out from the deluge immediately after the May 2, 2002, flood as this McDowell Street scene suggests. (Photograph by Rev. Tim Hairston.)

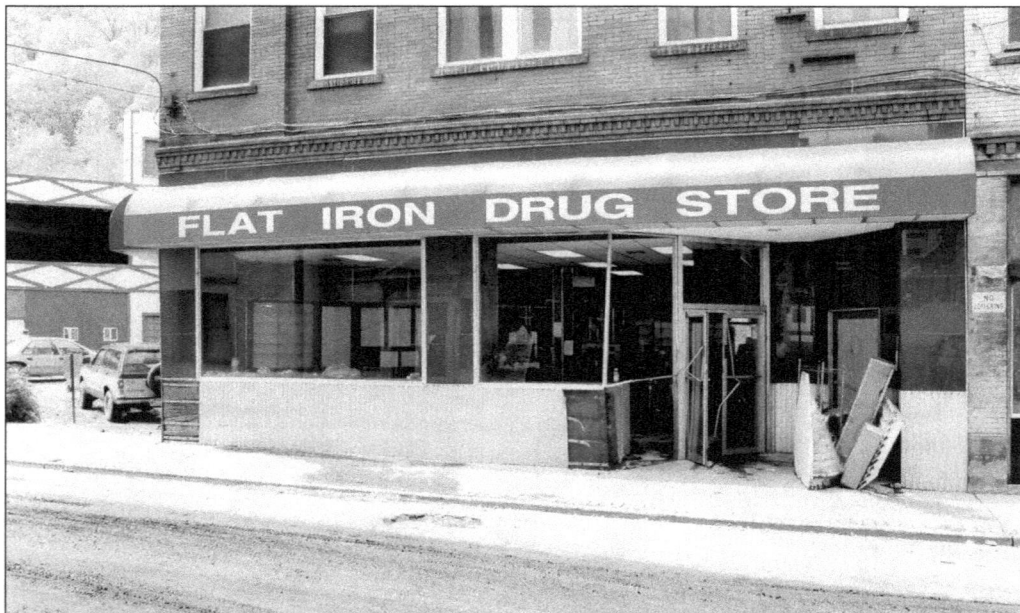

THE FAMOUS FLAT IRON. One of Welch's best-known businesses is the Flat Iron Drug Store. The 2002 flood had a devastating impact on the business, which has been a mainstay on McDowell Street since the city's early days. Flat Iron pharmacists Arvel Wyatt and Joe Monti didn't give up. They restored the business to better than its pre-flood condition. Wyatt started working at the pharmacy in November 1966. (Photograph by Rev. Tim Hairston.)

MAYOR MOORE. Welch Mayor Martha Moore was first elected to city council in 1985 and became the city's mayor the following year. While the city has faced enormous challenges during her two decades in office, Moore and the councils she has worked with have maintained a progressive, positive outlook and have accomplished a great deal. (Photograph by the author.)

YOU BE THE JUDGE. Rudolph J. "Rick" Murensky II served Welch in Charleston in the House of Delegates from 1980 to 1992 and continues to serve on the bench of the McDowell County Circuit Court. He was elected to his first eight-year term as judge in 2000. For a period of time, Murensky and his father, the late Rudolph J. "Rudy" Murensky, both sat on the bench at the same time—a rare occurrence in state judicial history. (Courtesy of Rick Murensky.)

WELCOME BACK. Even before the floods of 2001 and 2002, the City of Welch had been working on a revitalization plan aimed at sprucing up the community and capitalizing on its unique history. (Photograph by the author.)

NEW LOOK ON McDOWELL STREET. A new lighting project on McDowell Street completed in 2006 creates an old-time look in Welch. While the floods forced the demolition of some buildings in the city, others are gradually reemerging with businesses. (Photograph by the author.)

MASS COMMUNICATIONS. Radio Station WELC, located on a mountain overlooking the city, has been beaming a signal to the community for more than half a century. Sam Sidote, one of the founding owners of the radio station, can still be heard on the air almost every broadcast day. (Photograph by the author.)

LEGACY OF EXCELLENCE. The Sidotes—John; his wife, Vivian; and John's father, Sam Sidote— continue to broadcast news, sports, timely commercial messages, popular music, local programming of a religious nature, and much more to local listeners. When anything has an impact in Welch, McDowell County, or southern West Virginia and southwestern Virginia, WELC will be there. (Photograph by the author.)

NEW LOOK TO THE CITY. Several buildings of the downtown were razed after the 2002 flood, and by 2006, a new walled look along Elkhorn Creek is giving the city a different appearance. (Photograph by the author.)

YOU OUGHTTA BE IN PICTURES. After years of working with Marquee Cinemas to locate a theater in downtown Welch, the movies returned to the city in the spring of 2005. Welch had several theaters in the city during its heyday, but prior to the arrival of Marquee, the last picture house—the Pocahontas Theater—was destroyed by a fire on August 24, 1980. (Photograph by the author.)

TANKS FOR THE MEMORIES. Local artist Tom Acosta painted this water tank mural near the city overlook on the Welch bypass. Although the city has faced problems associated with population loss, economic doldrums, and natural disasters, it continues to hold out high hopes for the future. (Photograph by the author.)

A STERLING IDEA. For many years, the venerable Sterling Drive-In Restaurant on Stewart Street in Welch has been offering guests a choice of eating inside the restaurant or getting curbside service. (Photograph by the author.)

IN THE PRESENCE OF EAGLES. Students of the McDowell County Vocational and Technical Center created this incredible float honoring all McDowell County veterans—including those from the wars in Iraq and Afghanistan—and won first place in float competition at the annual Veterans Day Parade on November 11, 2005. When the huge eagle that topped the float was deployed to its position 10 feet above the float, pigeons that were observing the spectacle from rooftop perches on McDowell Street took flight. (Photograph by the author.)

WATER CONTROL. After the 2002 flood, McDowell County undertook a countywide streambed restoration program to remove decades of flash flood-borne debris from the streambeds. At the same time, the City of Welch worked with the state, Federal Emergency Management Agency, and the U.S. Army Corps of Engineers to address the flooding issue. The wall shown here under construction in Welch on the Elkhorn Creek is part of that project. (Photograph by the author.)

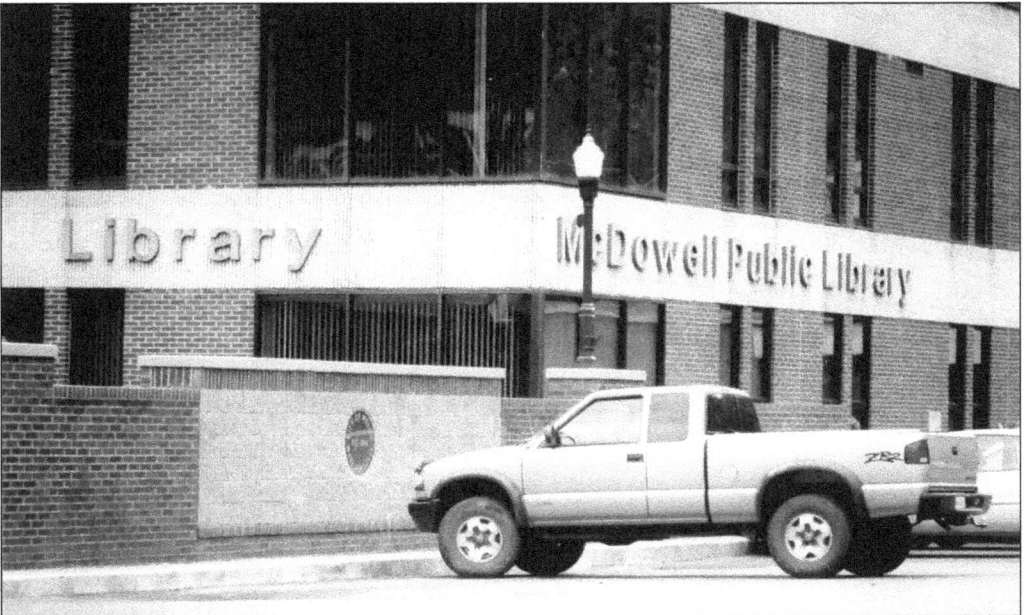

CHECK IT OUT. The McDowell County Public Library in Welch, as well as city hall, suffered extensive damages as a result of the 2002 flood, but thanks to the tireless efforts of staff and volunteers, both important services are back and functioning at full capacity. (Photograph by the author.)

127

Discover Thousands of Local History Books Featuring Millions of Vintage Images

Arcadia Publishing, the leading local history publisher in the United States, is committed to making history accessible and meaningful through publishing books that celebrate and preserve the heritage of America's people and places.

Find more books like this at
www.arcadiapublishing.com

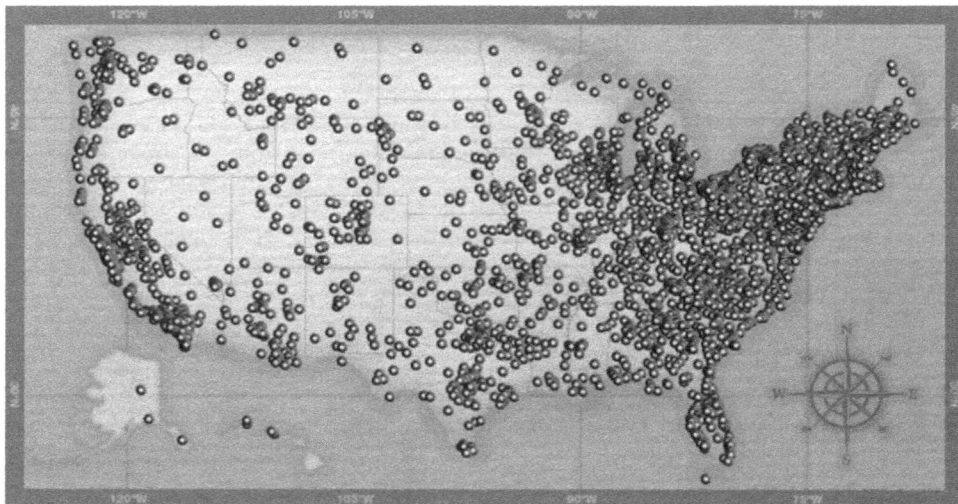

Search for your hometown history, your old stomping grounds, and even your favorite sports team.

www.ingramcontent.com/pod-product-compliance
Lightning Source LLC
Chambersburg PA
CBHW050609110426
42813CB00008B/2508